Easy Chinese Readings in 500 Characters

CHINESE MYTHS & FOLKTALES

Jian Zhu

中國 神話與 民间故事

This book will
quickly increase your ability to read Chinese

BIGI

Copyright

Chinese Myths and Folktales

ISBN 1-891107-00-3

Library of Congress Card Catalog Number   97-078193

First Edition

Written and edited by Jian Zhu
Translated by Molly Luethi
Cover and text design by Fong-Zhen Shiao
Cover illustration by Shih-Lun Tang
Chapter graphics by Shih-Lun Tang / Pita Ramirez / Chih-Hsiung Chien

Purchases, Inquiries, or Suggestions:

BIGI International USA Inc.

Publisher of Chinese and Computer Books

2501 San Pedro NE, Suite 208
Albuquerque, NM 87110
Telephone: 1-505-8301443
Fax: 1-505-8301448
Email: customer@bigiintl.com
http://www.bigiintl.com

Printed in Taiwan

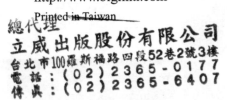

Preface

Chinese Myths and Folktales is one text in a series of innovative new Chinese readers written and edited specifically for students of Chinese who have had intensive beginning instruction (or the equivalent of four semesters of Chinese studies), and want to quickly improve their reading, writing, and speaking skills.

These books have been designed to help readers with fluency and proficiency within a format of rich cultural content aimed at providing readers with a greater understanding of the Chinese culture. The texts span a number of compelling topics ranging from ancient stories and traditions to current lifestyles and social change. We know of no other textbooks on the market encompassing such variety of topics and written in contemporary, up-to-date Chinese.

Readers of this series are presumed to have learned 500 basic characters from which to work. Unfortunately, when many students of Chinese have gained this level of competency, there are few materials to read to help them maintain their vocabulary and improve their reading skills. Our books have been written with careful attention to characters, expressions, grammar, and sentence structure to help readers achieve greater fluency. Cumbersome notes and explanations are unnecessary to understand the grammar in this series.

In addition to fluency, these texts are intended to help readers increase their vocabulary and use of common expressions. Each lesson contains approximately twenty to thirty new expressions for readers to learn. Some of these expressions may not be completely new, however, because they are combinations of characters readers already know, enabling readers to increase their vocabulary from chapter to chapter. For example, while readers will have already learned the characters for "big" and "person," when combined in the new expression as "big person," readers then learn the expression for "adult." There are hundreds of such examples in these books, as well as numerous current expressions now used in contemporary China.

One of the most powerful tools of language learning is repetition. Editors have worked diligently to ensure that these textbooks contain just the right amount of repetition of expressions and sentence structures. While these repetitions may at times appear redundant or excessive, many of these expressions are used frequently by the Chinese on a daily basis, and readers should gain a sense of their importance and variety of usage.

Readers' increased fluency and proficiency in Chinese is the editors' goal. We have also strived to produce books which make the study of Chinese both interesting and meaningful. Additional titles to enrich cultural understanding and language proficiency include Chinese Traditions and Festivals and Life in Beijing, both of which are in our series, Easy Chinese Readings in 500 Characters.

本書序言

　　<u>中國神話與民間故事</u>是 "<u>以五百生字輕鬆閱讀中文</u>" 系列叢書中的一本。這一系列中文閱讀叢書是為受過初步漢語教學訓練（相當於經過四個學期的中文課程學習），並希望迅速提高讀、寫和說中文能力的學生而編寫的。

　　為了使讀者更深更廣地了解中國文化，從而使讀者熟練掌握中文，這一系列叢書提供豐富的中國文化的文章。文章內容從中國的古代故事和習俗，直到現代中國的生活方式及社會變化的許多有趣的主題。我們知道現在的市場上看不到具有如此廣泛主題，而且使用當代中文表達的教科書。

　　這一系列叢書假定讀者有五百個中文生字的基礎，即可以開始閱讀這一系列叢書。現在有許多學生有五百字的中文能力，但不幸的是沒有可供他們閱讀的文章。這些作品將可以幫助學生維持他們已經學到的生字，並提高他們的閱讀能力。這一系列叢書的每一個生字、表達、語法和句子結構都經過仔細地推敲，使學生可以流暢閱讀。其中文章的文法簡單易懂，沒有加麻煩的注釋或解釋的必要。

　　除了有流暢性之外，這些文章還有計畫地增加讀者的詞彙，並使他們熟悉日常的中文習慣表達法。每一課包含了約二十到三十個讀者要學的新詞彙。它們並不是全新的詞，它們都是由讀者已經認識的字組成的。舉例來說，如讀者已經認識 "大" 和 "人" 兩個字，這兩個字組合起來就成了 "大人" 這個詞，放在文章中，讀者就可以學會。這些書中不但有數百個這樣的例子，而且還包含了數不清的現在中國人正使用的習慣表達法。就這樣，讓讀者逐漸地增加詞彙的數量。

　　重複是學習語言的最有力的工具之一。編輯們努力使一些表達法和句子結構在書中有恰到好處的多次重複。雖然有些重複的地方顯得多餘，但這些被重複的表達法，卻是中國人日常時時使用的，所以讀者可以從文中體會它們的重要性，並明白它們的多種用法。

　　我們努力讓讀者熟練掌握中文，同時也努力使文章有實質內容，讓讀者產生學習中文的興趣。像這樣能提高讀者文化理解能力和中文熟練程度的書籍，除了本書 "<u>中國神話與民間故事</u>" 之外，我們還有 "<u>中國的節日與民俗</u>" 以及 "<u>生活在北京</u>" 兩本，都屬於這一個 "<u>以五百生字輕鬆閱讀中文</u>" 的系列叢書。

CONTENT

目錄

第一章　盤古開天地和女媧造人

女媧造人

　　很久很久以前，在遠古的時候，世界上什麼東西都沒有。沒有山，沒有河，也沒有樹木，太陽和月亮也沒有。整個[1]的天和地都是在一起的，裏面黑黑的，外面看起來好像一個很大的蛋[2]。

　　又過了很久很久，這個蛋裏面慢慢生出來了一個人，他的名字叫盤古[3]。盤古是一個很高很大的人，他在這個蛋的裏面睡了一共一萬八千年，後來就起來了。當他起來的時候，覺得在蛋的裏面又黑又難過[4]，他很想出去看一看外面的天地。

他一次又一次地要出去，可是一點也沒有辦法[5]出去。他在蛋的裏面什麼也看不見，什麼也聽不見。蛋裏面的空氣也不好，這時盤古覺得越來越不舒服了。他就用了很大的力氣，要把蛋打開。突然，他聽到很大的"轟[6]"的一聲，最後蛋被打開了。

這個蛋並不是真正的蛋，而是上古的時候天和地的樣子。當蛋打開了以後，盤古就出來了。這時候，他覺得非常的舒服。蛋裏面那些淡[7]而輕的東西就慢慢的往天上去，變成了天。那些黑又重的東西就慢慢往地下來，變成了地。

但是，這時候的天地分得很近，盤古怕天地再回到一起變成蛋，就站在地上，把天舉[8]起來。他站在那裏，舉著天，舉了一萬八千年也沒有休息。在這一萬八千年裏，天變得越來越高，盤古也變得越來越高，最後天和地被分開了九萬里。這時的盤古已經非常累了。他再也沒有力氣，就突然"轟"的一聲倒[9]下去了。

盤古死了以後，他的四肢[10]變成了地上有名的大山，他的血[11]變成了江和河，他的眼睛變成了太陽和月亮，他身上的毛變成了地上的樹木，他口中的氣變成了天上和地上的風，傳說[12]最開始人們生活的世界就是這樣來的。

女媧造人

　　盤古開了天地以後，地上就有了這個美麗的世界。可是這個世界沒有什麼意思，因為地上一個人也沒有。有一天，一位美麗的女神[13]來到了這個地上，女神的名字叫女媧[14]。女媧看到地上一個人也沒有，心裏很不滿意。她覺得，這麼大的一個世界沒有人住，那有什麼意思呢？這時，女媧就想要造人[15]。當女媧來到一個水邊喝水的時候，她從水裏看到了自己美麗的樣子。她很高興，就在水邊用地上的泥土[16]做起人來。

　　女媧照著[17]自己的樣子做了一個小泥人，她把小泥人放到地上，向小泥人吹了一口氣，小泥人馬上就活了。女媧很高興，就把小泥人叫做 "人"。她又做了一些小泥人。結果，這些小泥人也都活了。他們都叫她 "媽媽！媽媽！" 女媧這時更高興了，她就一直不停地做起泥人來。十個、一百個、一千個…小泥人活了以後，就到別的地方去住了。

　　可是，女媧天天做泥人，白天做，晚上也做。累了也不能好好的休息。世界這麼大，泥人一個個的做太慢了。她想，什麼時候才能使人住滿整個大地呢？女媧就開始想辦法。她希望有一個更方便、更容易、和更快的方法來造人。

　　女媧想了一個好辦法。她用草[18]做成繩子[19]，把繩子上打上很多結[20]。她把打了結的繩子放到泥水裏，然後把繩子上的泥水灑[21]在地上，泥水一到地上就變成了人。原來，繩子上打的結是很特別的，從每一個結上出來的泥水都會變成一個人的樣子。而且，繩子上的結有的大，有的小。有的結很特別，有的結很一般[22]。這就是為什麼造出來的人，有的聰明，有的笨。有的人很好，也有的人不好。有男人，也有女人。那些笨的人和不好的人，就是女媧在不小心[23]的時候造出來的人。

女媧現在太高興了！她就一邊跑，一邊灑著泥水，她把泥水灑到了世界上的各個地方，地上很快就住滿了大大小小的人群[24]。從這個時候起，這些人群就生活在這個美麗的世界裏，一直到現在。

閱讀理解

一、 天和地原來是什麼樣子？

二、 天是怎樣來的？地是怎樣來的？

三、 天和地離開有多遠？

四、 盤古是怎樣死的？

五、 地上的世界最開始是怎樣來的？

六、 女媧是誰？

七、 女媧為什麼要造人？

八、 剛開始的時候，女媧是怎樣造人的？

九、 以這個傳說來說，為什麼世界上有不好的人？

生字

1	整個	zhěnggè	ㄓㄥˇ ㄍㄜ·	*whole*
2	蛋	dàn	ㄉㄢˋ	*egg*
3	盤古	pángǔ	ㄆㄢˊ ㄍㄨˇ	*legendary creator of heaven and earth.*
4	難過	nánguò	ㄋㄢˊ ㄍㄨㄛˋ	*sad; upset*
5	辦法	bànfǎ	ㄅㄢˋ ㄈㄚˇ	*way; method*
6	轟	hōng	ㄏㄨㄥ	*a big bang; boom*
7	淡	dàn	ㄉㄢˋ	*light; slight*
8	舉	jǔ	ㄐㄩˇ	*to hold up*
9	倒	dǎo	ㄉㄠˇ	*to fall*
10	四肢	sìzhī	ㄙˋ ㄓ	*four limbs*
11	血	xiě	ㄒㄧㄝˇ	*blood*
12	傳說	chuánshuō	ㄔㄨㄢˊ ㄕㄨㄛ	*according to legend*
13	神	shén	ㄕㄣˊ	*god*
14	女媧	nǚwā	ㄋㄩˇ ㄨㄚ	*legendary goddess who created man*
15	造人	zàorén	ㄗㄠˋ ㄖㄣˊ	*to create man*
16	泥土	nítǔ	ㄋㄧˊ ㄊㄨˇ	*soil*
17	照著	zhàozhe	ㄓㄠˋ ㄓㄜ·	*according to*
18	草	cǎo	ㄘㄠˇ	*grass*
19	繩子	shéngzi	ㄕㄥˊ ㄗ·	*rope*
20	結	jié	ㄐㄧㄝˊ	*a knot*
21	灑	sǎ	ㄙㄚˇ	*to spill*
22	一般	yībān	ㄧ ㄅㄢ	*ordinary*
23	不小心	bùxiǎoxīn	ㄅㄨˋ ㄒㄧㄠˇ ㄒㄧㄣ	*not careful*
24	人群	rénqún	ㄖㄣˊ ㄑㄩㄣˊ	*crowds*

第一章　盘古开天地和女娲造人

很久很久以前，在远古的时候，世界上什麽东西都没有。没有山，没有河，也没有树木，太阳和月亮也没有。整个[1]的天和地都是在一起的，里面黑黑的，外面看起来好像一个很大的蛋[2]。

又过了很久很久，这个蛋里面慢慢生出来了一个人，他的名字叫盘古[3]。盘古是一个很高很大的人，他在这个蛋的里面睡了一共一万八千年，後来就起来了。当他起来的时候，觉得在蛋的里面又黑又难过[4]，他很想出去看一看外面的天地。

他一次又一次地要出去，可是一点也没有办法[5]出去。他在蛋的里面什麽也看不见，什麽也听不见。蛋里面的空气也不好，这时盘古觉得越来越不舒服了。他就用了很大的力气，要把蛋打开。突然，他听到很大的"轰[6]"的一声，最後蛋被打开了。

这个蛋并不是真正的蛋，而是上古的时候天和地的样子。当蛋打开了以後，盘古就出来了。这时候，他觉得非常的舒服。蛋里面那些淡[7]而轻的东西就慢慢的往天上去，变成了天。那些黑又重的东西就慢慢往地下来，变成了地。

但是，这时候的天地分得很近，盘古怕天地再回到一起变成蛋，就站在地上，把天举[8]起来。他站在那里，举著天，举了一万八千年也没有休息。在这一万八千年里，天变得越来越高，盘古也变得越来越高，最後天和地被分开了九万里。这时的盘古已经非常累了。他再也没有力气，就突然"轰"的一声倒[9]下去了。

盘古死了以後，他的四肢[10]变成了地上有名的大山，他的血[11]变成了江和河，他的眼睛变成了太阳和月亮，他身上的毛变成了地上的树木，他口中的气变成了天上和地上的风，传说[12]最开始人们生活的世界就是这样来的。

女娲造人

盘古开了天地以後，地上就有了这个美丽的世界。可是这个世界没有什麽意思，因为地上一个人也没有。有一天，一位美丽的女神[13]来到了这个地上，女神的名字叫女娲[14]。女娲看到地上一个人也没有，心里很不满意。她觉得，这麽大的一个世界没有人住，那有什麽意思呢？这时，女娲就想要造人[15]。当女娲来到一个水边喝水的时候，她从水里看到了自己美丽的样子。她很高兴，就在水边用地上的泥土[16]做起人来。

女娲照著[17]自己的样子做了一个小泥人，她把小泥人放到地上，向小泥人吹了一口气，小泥人马上就活了。女娲很高兴，就把小泥人叫做"人"。她又做了一些小泥人。结果，这些小泥人也都活了。他们都叫她"妈妈！妈妈！"女娲这时更高兴了，她就一直不停地做起泥人来。十个、一百个、一千个…小泥人活了以後，就到别的地方去住了。

可是，女娲天天做泥人，白天做，晚上也做。累了也不能好好的休息。世界这麽大，泥人一个个的做太慢了。她想，什麽时候才能使人住满整个大地呢？女娲就开始想办法。她希望有一个更方便、更容易、和更快的方法来造人。

女娲想了一个好办法。她用草[18]做成绳子[19]，把绳子上打上很多结[20]。她把打了结的绳子放到泥水里，然後把绳子上的泥水洒[21]在地上，泥水一到地上就变成了人。原来，绳子上打的结是很特别的，从每一个结上出来的泥水都会变成一个人的样子。而且，绳子上的结有的大，有的小。有的结很特别，有的结很一般[22]。这就是为什麽造出来的人，有的聪明，有的笨。有的人很好，也有的人不好。有男人，也有女人。那些笨的人和不好的人，就是女娲在不小心[23]的时候造出来的人。

女娲现在太高兴了！她就一边跑，一边洒著泥水，她把泥水洒到了世界上的各个地方，地上很快就住满了大大小小的人群[24]。从这个时候起，这些人群就生活在这个美丽的世界里，一直到现在。

阅读理解

一、　天和地原来是什麽样子？

二、　天是怎样来的？地是怎样来的？

三、　天和地离开有多远？

四、　盘古是怎样死的？

五、　地上的世界最开始是怎样来的？

六、　女娲是谁？

七、　女娲为什麽要造人？

八、　刚开始的时候，女娲是怎样造人的？

九、　以这个传说来说，为什麽世界上有不好的人？

生字

1	整个	zhěnggè	whole
2	蛋	dàn	egg
3	盘古	pángǔ	legendary creator of heaven and earth.
4	难过	nánguò	sad; upset
5	办法	bànfǎ	way; method
6	轰	hōng	a big bang; boom
7	淡	dàn	light; slight
8	举	jǔ	to hold up
9	倒	dǎo	to fall
10	四肢	sìzhī	four limbs
11	血	xiě	blood
12	传说	chuánshuō	according to legend
13	神	shén	god
14	女娲	nǚwā	legendary goddess who created man
15	造人	zàorén	to create man
16	泥土	nítǔ	soil
17	照著	zhàozhe	according to
18	草	cǎo	grass
19	绳子	shéngzi	rope
20	结	jié	a knot
21	洒	sǎ	to spill
22	一般	yībān	ordinary
23	不小心	bùxiǎoxīn	not careful
24	人群	rénqún	crowds

Chapter 1   Pan Gu Separates Heaven and Earth and Nu Wa Creates Man

A long, long time ago, in the distant past, nothing at all existed in the world. No mountains, no rivers, no trees. There was not even a sun or a moon. Heaven and earth were one. It was very dark on the inside, and seen from the outside, it looked like a large egg.

As time passed, very slowly a person developed inside the egg, his name was Pan Gu. Pan Gu was very tall and very big. He spent 18,000 years sleeping inside the egg before he finally awoke. However, when he awoke he realized how dark and sad it was inside the egg. He really wanted to get out and have a look at the world outside.

He tried again and again to get out, but there was no way out. He couldn't see anything inside the egg, he couldn't hear anything either. The air inside the egg was not very good and he became more and more uncomfortable. So he made a great effort to try and split the egg open. Suddenly there was a great "Bang!" and the egg came apart.

This egg was not at all like a real egg, instead it was an image of the primeval world of heaven and earth. As soon as the egg was open, Pan Gu climbed out. That made him feel a lot better. All the thin, light objects inside the egg began to float slowly upward and became heaven. All the dark, heavy things sank down and became earth.

However, heaven and earth were still too close at that time. Pan Gu worried that they would rejoin and turn back into an egg, so he stood on the earth and held up the sky. He stood, holding up the sky for 18,000 years without resting. During those 18,000 years, the sky became very tall and Pan Gu became tall as well. In the end, heaven was separated from earth by 90,000 li. Pan Gu was very tired and had no more strength. Suddenly there was another loud "Bang!" and he fell over.

After Pan Gu died, his four limbs turned into famous mountains. His blood turned into rivers and his eyes turned into the sun and moon. The hair on his head turned into the trees growing on earth. The air in his mouth became the wind in the sky and on earth. According to legend, this is how the world of the first living beings was created.

Nu Wa Creates Man

After Pan Gu had separated heaven and earth, a beautiful world existed on earth. However, it was not an interesting place because there were no people. One day a beautiful goddess named Nu Wa came to earth. When Nu Wa saw that there were no people around she was not pleased. How can such a big place with no people in it be of any interest, she wondered. So she decided to create people. When Nu Wa drank water along the shore, she saw her own beautiful reflection in the water. She was so happy that she took the clay at the edge of the water and from it she created a person.

Nu Wa made a small clay person who looked just like her. She placed the clay person on the ground and blew a puff of air into the figure. The little clay person immediately came to life and Nu Wa was very happy and called this little clay person 'Human.' She made more little clay people and they all came to life. They all called her 'Mama, Mama.' This made Nu Wa even happier and she could not stop creating more clay people. She made ten, then one hundred, then one thousand... As soon as the little clay figures came to life, they went off to live in another place.

Nu Wa continued making clay figures; she made them during the day and she made them at night. Even when she was tired she couldn't rest properly. The world was so big, making clay people one by one was simply too slow. She wondered when she would ever be able to fill the earth with people. She started thinking about new methods. She wanted to find a more convenient, easier, and faster way to create people.

She came up with a good idea. She used grass to make a rope, and then she tied many knots into the rope. Then she dipped the rope into mud and let the water from the rope drip onto the ground. As soon as the mud touched the ground, it turned into a person. Each knot that was tied into the rope was quite different, and the mud that came out of each knot turned into a human figure. What is more, some knots were large, some small. Some knots were particular and others were quite ordinary. That is why some of the people were created clever, others were stupid. Some of the people ended up being good, others were not so good. Some were males and some were females. The ones who ended up being stupid or evil were the ones who had been created when Nu Wa wasn't paying attention.

Nu Wa was very pleased. She leaped around, spilling mud all over the world. The earth was soon filled with bigger and smaller groups of people. From then on, up until today, this multitude of people have lived on this beautiful earth.

第二章　后羿射日[1]和大禹治水

后羿射日

　　傳說遠古的時候，天上的神生了十個小太陽，這十個小太陽都住在天上一個美麗的湖邊，他們每天都喜歡在湖裏玩。當十個小太陽下到湖裏去玩的時候，湖裏的水就會變得很熱很熱。到了晚上，小太陽們就睡在湖邊的大樹上。大樹上住了一隻[2]紅紅的火雞[3]，每天早上火雞就把小太陽們叫起來。小太陽們天天玩得很高興。他們每一天的生活都是很好玩，很熱鬧的，因爲他們身上有太多的光和熱。

　幾萬年過去了，小太陽們的媽媽有一天對孩子們說："我們要把光和熱送到大地上去。"孩子們聽了，都非常高興。第二天一早，太陽媽媽就帶著大兒子出發[4]了，其他的小太陽就在家裏玩。媽媽和大兒子坐著龍車[5]像飛一樣的在天上跑，從東到西一共跑了五十多萬里，把光和熱帶給了大地上的樹木、動物[6]、和人類[7]。

　第三天早上，媽媽又帶著第二個兒子坐著龍車，從東到西地跑去，第四天，又是帶另一個兒子去…。每一天，媽媽就是這樣帶著一個兒子，不停的[8]在天上跑著，把光和熱帶給大地。大地因爲有了太陽的光和熱，樹木就變綠了，花也變紅了，人們的生活就變得有希望了。

　一天，吃完晚飯的時候，十個小太陽坐在一起喝茶，他們高興地談起每天看到的事情。他們看到的最有意思的事情，都是發生在人類各個地方的事情，如結婚、生孩子、和過年等等。可是，他們覺得沒有意思的是，媽媽每天都要跟著他們一起去。

　十個小太陽裏，有一個弟弟是最調皮[9]的。他說："明天我們一起出去，不讓媽媽知道，好嗎？"大家就都同意了。也許所有的小孩子都是一樣，不喜歡聽爸爸媽媽的話，不喜歡什麼事都照爸爸媽媽說的去做。第二天很早很早的時候，媽媽還沒有起來，十個小太陽就已經坐著龍車一起出發了。媽媽後來知道的時候，已經太晚了。

十個小太陽們離大地越來越近了。想到媽媽不在一起，自己可以隨便玩，他們高興得又唱又跳，好像在自己的家裏玩一樣。可是，這一下麻煩了。大地上的樹木和花草熱得快死了。河水也快乾[10]了，動物都熱得不知道該躲到哪裏。人們也熱得非常難過，一點力氣也沒有。很快地，許多動物和人們開始死去。

這時候，有一個皇帝，大聲地請小太陽們馬上離開，使大地上的樹木、動物、和人可以活下去。可是，小太陽們一點也不聽，反而玩得更高興。皇帝一點辦法也沒有了。突然，他想到了一個人。這個人的名字叫后羿[11]，他的力氣很大，也很會射箭[12]，他可以射中幾百里以外的一片樹葉。

后羿聽說後，就決定去幫助皇帝，他和家裏人說了再見，就出發了。他一路上看到許多死去的樹木、動物、和人，心裏十分難過和生氣。他來到一個很高的山上，對十個小太陽說話，要他們馬上離開這裏。可是后羿的這些話一點也沒有用。小太陽們既不回去，也不[13]回答他。這時，后羿就決定把小太陽們射下來。他對著一個小太陽，一箭射去。只聽"轟"的一聲，一個小太陽被射下來了。其它的小太陽還沒有明白是怎麼一回事[14]，又聽見"轟！轟！"的幾聲，兩三個小太陽又接著掉[15]下來了。剩下的小太陽，有的想要跑，

有的非常生氣，想要燒[16]死后羿。結果，他們一個又一個的
被后羿射下來了。射下來的小太陽掉到了大海裏，變成了海
邊的大石頭[17]和海中的小島[18]。

現在，天上只剩下了一個小太陽，他怕自己也被射下來，
就哭[19]了起來。這時，大地上下起了大雨，地上的樹木、花
草[20]又活過來了。所有的動物和人們都跑出來，高興得唱[21]起
歌[22]來，跳起舞[23]來。后羿又要射最後的這一個小太陽時，突
然聽見有人喊[24]著說：“人們需要太陽的光和熱，留下[25]他幫
助人類吧！”后羿聽了，就不再射了。因為他射得正高興的
時候，就忘了人類還需要太陽。天上掉下了九個太陽，地上
的天氣又變得好起來了。從那以後，天上就只剩下一個太陽
了。

大禹[26]治水[27]

傳說遠古的時候，住在地上的人變得越來越不好了，人
手上做的和心裏想的，都是天上的神所不喜歡的事情。人在
世界上沒有真正的平安。天上的神看見了這些，非常生氣，
就放大水到地上來。天上的神這樣做，是要地上的人們知道，
他們做的事情都是不對的，是神很不喜歡的。那時，到處都
是很大的大水，一共二十二年。

因為到處是水，又沒有住的地方，也沒有什麼吃的，所
以地上的生活很不容易。人們都離開了自己的家，往高山上
去住。可是，雖然人們住到了高山上，天下的大水還是一直

不離去。這時，就有一個很有能力的人出來，要帶著天下的人們一起來治水。這個人的名字叫大禹。

　　大禹的父親以前也是治水的，後來他父親死了，治水的工作還沒有完。人們就希望他的兒子大禹能把治水的工作接下去。大禹和人民一起治水，整整花了十三年。這樣[28]，大禹就接著做了他父親的工作，帶著人們一起治水。他們在地上開了許許多多的大小水道，讓大水流到[29]小河裏，小河裏的水又流到大河裏，大河最後流到大海裏。用這個方法，大水慢慢地就流出去了。從那以後，地上就不再有大水了。人們又開始了新的生活。

閱讀理解：

一、　太陽一家的生活是怎樣的？

二、　小太陽們給了人類什麼麻煩？

三、　后羿是誰？他為人類做了什麼事？

四、　天上的另外九個太陽到什麼地方去了？

五、　海裏的石頭和島是從那裏來的？

六、　大禹是誰？

七、　地上為什麼會有大水？

八、　大禹是怎樣治水的？

九、　大禹的父親和大禹一共治水治了多少年？

生字

¹ 射日	shèrì	ㄕㄜˋ ㄖˋ	to shoot the sun
² 一隻	yīzhī	ㄧ ㄓ	measure word for turkey
³ 火雞	huǒjī	ㄏㄨㄛˇ ㄐㄧ	turkey
⁴ 出發	chūfā	ㄔㄨ ㄈㄚ	to set out
⁵ 龍車	lóngchē	ㄌㄨㄥˊ ㄔㄜ	dragon cart
⁶ 動物	dòngwù	ㄉㄨㄥˋ ㄨˋ	animals
⁷ 人類	rénlèi	ㄖㄣˊ ㄌㄟˋ	people
⁸ 不停的	bùtíngde	ㄅㄨˋ ㄊㄧㄥˊ ㄉㄜ·	without interruption
⁹ 調皮	tiáopí	ㄊㄧㄠˊ ㄆㄧˊ	naughty
¹⁰ 乾	gān	ㄍㄢ	dry
¹¹ 后羿	hòuyì	ㄏㄡˋ ㄧˋ	name of the hero who shoots down the suns
¹² 射箭	shèjiàn	ㄕㄜˋ ㄐㄧㄢˋ	to shoot arrows
¹³ 既不⋯也不⋯	jìbù⋯yěbù⋯	ㄐㄧˋ ㄅㄨˋ ⋯ㄧㄝˇ ㄅㄨˋ ⋯	neither⋯nor⋯
¹⁴ 怎麼一回事	zěmoyīhuíshì	ㄗㄜˇ ㄇㄛ· ㄧ ㄏㄨㄟˊ ㄕˋ	what is happening
¹⁵ 掉	diào	ㄉㄧㄠˋ	to fall
¹⁶ 燒	shāo	ㄕㄠ	to burn
¹⁷ 石頭	shítóu	ㄕˊ ㄊㄡˊ	rock
¹⁸ 小島	xiǎodǎo	ㄒㄧㄠˇ ㄉㄠˇ	island
¹⁹ 哭	kū	ㄎㄨ	to cry
²⁰ 花草	huācǎo	ㄏㄨㄚ ㄘㄠˇ	flowers and grass
²¹ 唱	chàng	ㄔㄤˋ	to sing
²² 歌	gē	ㄍㄜ	song

²³ 跳起舞來	tiàoqǐwǔlái	ㄊㄧㄠˋ ㄑㄧˇ ㄨˇ ㄌㄞˊ	*to begin to dance*
²⁴ 喊	hǎn	ㄏㄢˇ	*to shout*
²⁵ 留下	liúxià	ㄌㄧㄡˊ ㄒㄧㄚˋ	*to leave behind*
²⁶ 大禹	dàyǔ	ㄉㄚˋ ㄩˇ	*name of the hero who controlled the flood*
²⁷ 治水	zhìshuǐ	ㄓˋ ㄕㄨㄟˇ	*to control the water*
²⁸ 這樣	zhèyàng	ㄓㄜˋ ㄧㄤˋ	*like this; thus*
²⁹ 流到	liúdào	ㄌㄧㄡˊ ㄉㄠˋ	*to flow to*

第二章　后羿射日[1]和大禹治水

　　传说远古的时候，天上的神生了十个小太阳，这十个小太阳都住在天上一个美丽的湖边，他们每天都喜欢在湖里玩。当十个小太阳下到湖里去玩的时候，湖里的水就会变得很热很热。到了晚上，小太阳们就睡在湖边的大树上。大树上住了一只[2]红红的火鸡[3]，每天早上火鸡就把小太阳们叫起来。小太阳们天天玩得很高兴。他们每一天的生活都是很好玩，很热闹的，因为他们身上有太多的光和热。

　　几万年过去了，小太阳们的妈妈有一天对孩子们说："我们要把光和热送到大地上去。"孩子们听了，都非常高兴。第二天一早，太阳妈妈就带著大儿子出发[4]了，其他的小太阳就在家里玩。妈妈和大儿子坐著龙车[5]像飞一样的在天上跑，从东到西一共跑了五十多万里，把光和热带给了大地上的树木、动物[6]、和人类[7]。

　　第三天早上，妈妈又带著第二个儿子坐著龙车，从东到西地跑去，第四天，又是带另一个儿子去…。每一天，妈妈就是这样带著一个儿子，不停的[8]在天上跑著，把光和热带给大地。

大地因为有了太阳的光和热，树木就变绿了，花也变红了，人们的生活就变得有希望了。

一天，吃完晚饭的时候，十个小太阳坐在一起喝茶，他们高兴地谈起每天看到的事情。他们看到的最有意思的事情，都是发生在人类各个地方的事情，如结婚、生孩子、和过年等等。可是，他们觉得没有意思的是，妈妈每天都要跟著他们一起去。

十个小太阳里，有一个弟弟是最调皮[9]的。他说："明天我们一起出去，不让妈妈知道，好吗？"大家就都同意了。也许所有的小孩子都是一样，不喜欢听爸爸妈妈的话，不喜欢什麼事都照爸爸妈妈说的去做。第二天很早很早的时候，妈妈还没有起来，十个小太阳就已经坐著龙车一起出发了。妈妈後来知道的时候，已经太晚了。

十个小太阳们离大地越来越近了。想到妈妈不在一起，自己可以随便玩，他们高兴得又唱又跳，好像在自己的家里玩一样。可是，这一下麻烦了。大地上的树木和花草热得快死了。河水也快乾[10]了，动物都热得不知道该躲到哪里。人们也热得非常难过，一点力气也没有。很快地，许多动物和人们开始死去。

这时候，有一个皇帝，大声地请小太阳们马上离开，使大地上的树木、动物、和人可以活下去。可是，小太阳们一点也不听，反而玩得更高兴。皇帝一点办法也没有了。突然，他想到了一个人。这个人的名字叫后羿[11]，他的力气很大，也很会射箭[12]，他可以射中几百里以外的一片树叶。

后羿听说後，就决定去帮助皇帝，他和家里人说了再见，就出发了。他一路上看到许多死去的树木、动物、和人，心里十分难过和生气。他来到一个很高的山上，对十个小太阳说话，要他们马上离开这里。可是后羿的这些话一点也没有用。小太阳们既不回去，也不[13]回答他。这时，后羿就决定把小太阳们射下来。他对著一个小太阳，一箭射去。只听"轰"的一声，一个小太阳被射下来了。其它的小太阳还没有明白是怎麼一回事[14]，又听见"轰！轰！"的几声，两三个小太阳又接著掉[15]下来了。剩下的小太阳，有的想要跑，有的非常生气，想要烧[16]死后羿。结果，他们一个又一个的被后羿射下来了。射下来的小太阳掉到了大海里，变成了海边的大石头[17]和海中的小岛[18]。

现在，天上只剩下了一个小太阳，他怕自己也被射下来，就哭[19]了起来。这时，大地上下起了大雨，地上的树木、花草[20]又活过来了。所有的动物和人们都跑出来，高兴得唱[21]起歌[22]来，跳起舞[23]来。后羿又要射最后的这一个小太阳时，突然听见有人喊[24]著说："人们需要太阳的光和热，留下[25]他帮助人类吧！"后羿听了，就不再射了。因为他射得正高兴的时候，就忘了人类还需要太阳。天上掉下了九个太阳，地上的天气又变得好起来了。从那以后，天上就只剩下一个太阳了。

大禹²⁶治水²⁷

传说远古的时候，住在地上的人变得越来越不好了，人手上做的和心里想的，都是天上的神所不喜欢的事情。人在世界上没有真正的平安。天上的神看见了这些，非常生气，就放大水到地上来。天上的神这样做，是要地上的人们知道，他们做的事情都是不对的，是神很不喜欢的。那时，到处都是很大的大水，一共二十二年。

因为到处是水，又没有住的地方，也没有什麽吃的，所以地上的生活很不容易。人们都离开了自己的家，往高山上去住。可是，虽然人们住到了高山上，天下的大水还是一直不离去。这时，就有一个很有能力的人出来，要带著天下的人们一起来治水。这个人的名字叫大禹。

大禹的父亲以前也是治水的，後来他父亲死了，治水的工作还没有完。人们就希望他的儿子大禹能把治水的工作接下去。大禹和人民一起治水，整整花了十三年。这样²⁸，大禹就接著做了他父亲的工作，带著人们一起治水。他们在地上开了许许多多的大小水道，让大水流到²⁹小河里，小河里的水又流到大河里，大河最後流到大海里。用这个方法，大水慢慢地就流出去了。从那以後，地上就不再有大水了。人们又开始了新的生活。

阅读理解：

一、 太阳一家的生活是怎样的？

二、 小太阳们给了人类什麽麻烦？

三、 后羿是谁？他为人类做了什麽事？

四、 天上的另外九个太阳到什麽地方去了？

五、 海里的石头和岛是从那里来的？

六、 大禹是谁？

七、 地上为什麽会有大水？

八、 大禹是怎样治水的？

九、 大禹的父亲和大禹一共治水治了多少年？

生字

1	射日	shèrì	to shoot the sun
2	一只	yīzhī	measure word for turkey
3	火鸡	huǒjī	turkey
4	出发	chūfā	to set out
5	龙车	lóngchē	dragon cart
6	动物	dòngwù	animals
7	人类	rénlèi	people
8	不停的	bùtíngde	without interruption
9	调皮	tiáopí	naughty
10	乾	gān	dry
11	后羿	hòuyì	name of the hero who shoots down the suns
12	射箭	shèjiàn	to shoot arrows
13	既不…也不…	jìbù…yěbù…	neither…nor…
14	怎麼一回事	zěmoyīhuíshì	what is happening
15	掉	diào	to fall
16	烧	shāo	to burn
17	石头	shítóu	rock
18	小岛	xiǎodǎo	island
19	哭	kū	to cry
20	花草	huācǎo	flowers and grass
21	唱	chàng	to sing
22	歌	gē	song
23	跳起舞来	tiàoqǐwǔlái	to begin to dance
24	喊	hǎn	to shout
25	留下	liúxià	to leave behind
26	大禹	dàyǔ	name of the hero who controlled the flood
27	治水	zhìshuǐ	to control the water
28	这样	zhèyàng	like this; thus
29	流到	liúdào	to flow to

Chapter 2   Hou Yi Shoots the Sun and Da Yu

Controls the Water

According to an ancient legend, god in heaven gave birth to ten little suns. These ten suns lived next to a lovely lake up in the sky. They enjoyed playing in the lake everyday. When the ten suns played in the lake, the water in the lake became very, very hot. At nighttime the suns slept in a big tree next to the lake. A bright red turkey lived in that tree and every morning the turkey woke the little suns up. The little suns played happily everyday. Their life was fun and lively because their bodies were filled with light and warmth.

One day, after many tens of thousands of years, the mother sun said to her children, "We are going to bring some light and warmth to earth." The children were excited to hear this. On the morning of the second day, the mother sun set off with her eldest child while the other little suns stayed home and played. The mother sun and her eldest traveled through the sky on a dragon cart, it seemed as if they were flying across heaven. From east to west they traveled over 500,000 li, bringing light and warmth to the trees, the animals, and the people on earth.

On the third day, the mother sun took her second eldest child and traveled through heaven from east to west on the dragon cart. On the fourth day, she took another child. Everyday, without interruption, the mother took one of her children and traveled through heaven bringing light and warmth to earth. Because the earth got so much light and warmth, the trees started turning green, the flowers turned red, and the people's lives were filled with hope.

One day, after eating their dinner, the ten little suns were sitting around drinking tea. They were telling each other the things they had seen. The most interesting things they had seen had happened where humans lived. A wedding, for example, or the birth of a child, or a New Year celebration, etc. What they didn't like was that their mother wanted to accompany them everyday.

One of the younger brothers among the ten little suns, who was also the naughtiest, said, "How about going out together tomorrow and not telling mother about it?" The others all agreed. Children everywhere are probably like that, they don't always obey their parents, and they don't always like doing things according to their parents. Very early the next morning, when mother wasn't yet up, the ten little suns got onto the dragon cart and set off. Later on, when their mother discovered what had happened, it was already too late.

The ten little suns came nearer and nearer to earth. Because their mother wasn't with them, they felt free to play as they wished. They sang and jumped and felt as if they were in their own backyard. However, that is how the troubles began. The trees and flowers on earth began to burn up from the heat. The water in the rivers dried up; the animals were very hot and didn't know where they could hide. The people had a terrible time and lost all their strength because of the heat. Very soon many animals and humans began to die.

The emperor who lived at that time told the little suns in a loud voice to leave to allow the trees, the animals, and the humans to live. But the little suns did not listen. On the contrary, they played even more. The emperor didn't know what to do. Suddenly he thought of something, he thought of Hou Yi, who was very strong and also a very good archer. Hou Yi could shoot a particular leaf off a tree that was several hundred li away.

Hou Yi heard about the difficulties and decided to help the emperor. He said good-bye to his family and left. Along the way he saw many dead trees, dead animals, and dead people; he felt both sorry and angry. When he arrived on the summit of a very tall mountain, he spoke to the ten little suns and asked them to leave right away. However, Hou Yi's speech was of no use. Not only did the suns not leave, they didn't answer him either. So Hou Yi decided to shoot the little suns out of the sky. He aimed at one of the suns and shot an arrow at it. Just one "Bang!" was heard and one of the suns was shot down. The other little suns had not yet seen what was happening when "Bang! Bang!" a second and third followed and fell. Some of the remaining suns wanted to escape, others were angry and wanted to burn Hou Yi to death. One by one, Hou Yi shot them down. The little suns fell into the ocean where they turned into big rocks along the shore, or islands in the sea.

Now there was only one sun left in the sky. It was afraid that it, too, would be shot down, and it started to cry. Rain began to fall on earth and all the trees, the flowers, and grass came back to life. The animals and the people all came running; they were so happy that they started to sing and dance. And when Hou Yi wanted to shoot down the last of the little suns, he heard someone shout, "People need light and warmth from the sun, leave it up there and it will help mankind!" When Hou Yi heard these words, he didn't shoot again. Because he had been so involved with shooting down the other suns, he had forgotten that human beings need the sun. After the nine little suns had been shot down, the weather on earth became fine again. From that day on, there has only been one sun in the sky.

Da Yu Controls the Water

In ancient legendary times, the people living on earth became more and more evil. What people did with their hands and thought in their hearts were things god up in heaven didn't like. There was no real peace on earth. When god saw this, he got very angry and sent a flood to earth. God did this in order to let the people know that what they did was wrong and that he did not like it. The flood covered everything and it lasted twenty-two years.

Because there was water everywhere, there was no place to live, no food to eat. Life on earth became very difficult. All the people fled their homes to live in the mountains. However, even though the people fled to the mountains, the flood did not go away. At that time, a very capable man appeared who wanted to lead the people in controlling the water. This man's name was Da Yu. In his lifetime, Da Yu's father had worked on regulating the rivers and waterways. When he died, his work was not yet finished. The people hoped that his son, Da Yu, would continue his father's work. Together with all the people, Da Yu spent thirteen years regulating the waterways. So Da Yu ended up continuing his father's work, regulating the waterways together with all the people. They opened up many narrow waterways to allow the flood waters to flow into the small rivers, the water in the small rivers then flowed into larger rivers, and the larger rivers ended up flowing into the ocean. By using this method, the flood waters slowly flowed away. Since that time, there has not been a flood on earth and the people started living a new life.

第三章　黃帝中國和倉頡造字

倉頡造字

　　黃帝[1]不是歷史上的所叫的"皇帝"。皇帝是一個國家的王，整個國家都是他的；但黃帝是傳說中的神，整個天地都是他的。他是天上最大的神，又是地上所有的自然、動物、和人類的王。傳說黃帝有四個臉，時時看著東南西北的每一個方向。所以，天上和地上的每一件事情黃帝都知道。

　　黃帝住在天上，但是他也常常到地上來。他是天上的王，可是他也幫助住在地上的人們，關心[2]他們的生活和幸福。傳說黃帝每次從天上下來的時候，是坐在一條龍的背上[3]。他來到地上時，常常住在東方的一個高山上。那時候，東方還沒有國家，可是住在東方的人有很多很多。黃帝就幫助東方人開始了第一個國家，叫做中國。意思是說，這是黃帝住的國家。因爲黃帝有東西南北四個臉，所以黃帝住的地方，永遠是世界的中心。

傳說黃帝經常幫助中國的人民，給他們幸福和平安的生活。可是黃帝給中國人的最大影響，是幫助他們開始國家和社會的生活。黃帝是一位很有能力的神，他身邊[4]還有七十位有能力的神來幫助他。黃帝和他身邊的神就幫助中國人，教他們用火[5]來燒飯吃。中國人會用火以後，就開始有了文化。

黃帝和他身邊的神，還幫助了中國人許多的事情，教他們學會穿[6]衣服[7]。穿衣服也是文化的開始，因爲穿上了衣服，人和動物就不一樣了。黃帝還教了中國人很多的東西，他把音樂、醫藥[8]、和漢字帶給了中國人。因爲黃帝的幫助，東方就有了第一個國家。這就是今天的中國。

因爲黃帝對中國人的幫助很大，影響了中國幾千年的文化，所以中國人常常說自己是黃帝的後代[9]，他們覺得傳說中的黃帝就是中國人的祖先[10]。因爲傳說中黃帝常常坐著龍走來走去，所以，中國人又喜歡用龍來表現中國的文化和歷史上發生的事情。比如，中國人常常喜歡用龍來代表長城[11]和黃河[12]。

　　黃帝在世上的時候，天上的神和地上的人是可以隨便來往[13]的。神到地上來和人到天上去都是很容易的。可是，傳說後來黃帝回到天上去了。以後，天和地的路就不見了。天上的神就不容易再到地上來，地上的人也不容易到天上去了。

倉頡造字

　　倉頡是黃帝身邊的一位神。他的工作是把每天發生的大事和小事都記下來，讓人們可以知道和學習。可是那時候還沒有發明文字[14]。倉頡記下來的事情沒有一個人可以看懂。所以，倉頡就想辦法，要發明一種文字。他希望用這種文字來記事[15]和寫歷史，讓後來的人可以知道以前發生過的事情。所以，倉頡每天就在想這件事情。

　　在遠古的時候，中國人記事的方法，是在繩子上打結。每次發生什麼事情，就在繩子上打一個結。大事就打一個大結，小事就打一個小結。可是，這個記事的方法有一個麻煩。就是日子久了以後，雖然可以知道發生了多少事情，可是沒有辦法知道發生了什麼事情。

　　後來，有人就用畫畫的方法來記事。每一天發生的事情都畫在木頭[16]上或石頭上，因為那時候還沒有紙和筆。記在木頭或石頭上的事情比記在繩子上好多了。記事的人現在可以告訴別人過去發生了什麼事。看見這些畫的人，大概也能猜出來過去發生了什麼事。

可是，畫畫也有很多的麻煩。因爲在木頭和石頭上畫畫是很不容易的。而且，記下一件事情有的時候要畫幾個畫。所以，記事情要花很多的時間，是一件很累人[17]的工作。有的時候，即使每天發生的事情並不重要，可是記事的工作卻變成很重要。每天的事情也許並不忙，可是記事的人卻變成了最忙的人了。

倉頡看見人們記事不容易，就天天想辦法，要發明文字。他希望有了文字，人們記事會變得方便一些。後來的人也可以看得懂，以前古時候的人記下來的歷史。所以，倉頡就天天想這件事情。有一天，倉頡看見了一隻很大很大的烏龜[18]。這個烏龜年紀很大了，它的背上已經有了很多的花紋[19]，就像人老了，臉上有很多的皺紋[20]一樣。

倉頡走近一看，看見有的花紋像山，有的花紋像水，又有的花紋像樹。傳說，倉頡有四隻眼睛，所以看東西和別人不一樣。倉頡這時想：爲什麼不能用簡單的線條[21]來代表要畫的東西和事情呢？這樣，記事就變得很容易了。如果能把這種用線條畫畫的方法，教給後來的人，大家就不都能看懂文字了嗎？

倉頡就這樣開始造起字來。他用最簡單的線條來代表要畫的東西的樣子。這些就是最早的漢字，也叫"象形文字[22]"。倉頡造了多少個漢字呢？這個問題沒有人能知道。後來的漢人又接著倉頡繼續造字[23]。語言學家一般認爲，現代[24]

的漢字一共有六萬多個，常用的漢字差不多有三千多個。有了漢字，中國文化就有了很大的變化。紙和筆也就發明出來了。漢字後來也流傳[25]到了日本和東南亞[26]的一些國家。

閱讀理解：

一、　黃帝爲什麼是四個臉？

二、　黃帝給中國人最大的影響是什麼？

三、　中國人是怎樣開始自己的文化的？

四、　爲什麼說中國人是黃帝的後代？

五、　中國文化爲什麼喜歡用龍來代表？

六、　倉頡的主要工作是什麼？

七、　古時候的人們用什麼方法來記事？

八、　倉頡是怎樣發明文字的？

生字

[1] 黃帝	huángdì	ㄏㄨㄤˊ ㄉㄧˋ	*the Yellow Emperor*
[2] 關心	guānxīn	ㄍㄨㄢ ㄒㄧㄣ	*to be concerned about*
[3] 背上	bèishàng	ㄅㄟˋ ㄕㄤˋ	*on the back*
[4] 身邊	shēnbiān	ㄕㄣ ㄅㄧㄢ	*at his side*
[5] 火	huǒ	ㄏㄨㄛˇ	*fire*
[6] 穿	chuān	ㄔㄨㄢ	*to wear*
[7] 衣服	yīfú	ㄧ ㄈㄨˊ	*clothes*

[8] 醫藥	yīyào	ㄧ ㄧㄠˋ	*medicine*
[9] 後代	hòudài	ㄏㄡˋ ㄉㄞˋ	*Posterity; later generations*
[10] 祖先	zǔxiān	ㄗㄨˇ ㄒㄧㄢ	*ancestors*
[11] 長城	chángchéng	ㄔㄤˊ ㄔㄥˊ	*the Great Wall*
[12] 黃河	huánghé	ㄏㄨㄤˊ ㄏㄜˊ	*the Yellow River*
[13] 來往	láiwǎng	ㄌㄞˊ ㄨㄤˇ	*to have contact*
[14] 文字	wénzì	ㄨㄣˊ ㄗˋ	*writing*
[15] 記事	jìshì	ㄐㄧˋ ㄕˋ	*to record*
[16] 木頭	mùtóu	ㄇㄨˋ ㄊㄡˊ	*wood*
[17] 累人	lèirén	ㄌㄟˋ ㄖㄣˊ	*to be exhausting*
[18] 烏龜	wūguī	ㄨ ㄍㄨㄟ	*tortoise*
[19] 花紋	huāwén	ㄏㄨㄚ ㄨㄣˊ	*pattern; design*
[20] 皺紋	zhòuwén	ㄓㄡˋ ㄨㄣˊ	*wrinkles*
[21] 線條	xiàntiáo	ㄒㄧㄢˋ ㄊㄧㄠˊ	*lines*
[22] 象形文字	xiàngxíngwénzì	ㄒㄧㄤˋ ㄒㄧㄥˊ ㄨㄣˊ ㄗˋ	*pictograph*
[23] 造字	zàozì	ㄗㄠˋ ㄗˋ	*to create words*
[24] 現代	xiàndài	ㄒㄧㄢˋ ㄉㄞˋ	*modern*
[25] 流傳	liúchuán	ㄌㄧㄡˊ ㄔㄨㄢˊ	*to spread; to hand down*
[26] 東南亞	dōngnányǎ	ㄉㄨㄥ ㄋㄢˊ ㄧㄚˇ	*Southeast Asia*

第三章　黄帝中国和仓颉造字

　　黄帝[1]不是历史上的所叫的"皇帝"。皇帝是一个国家的王，整个国家都是他的；但黄帝是传说中的神，整个天地都是他的。他是天上最大的神，又是地上所有的自然、动物、和人类的王。传说黄帝有四个脸，时时看著东南西北的每一个方向。所以，天上和地上的每一件事情黄帝都知道。

　　黄帝住在天上，但是他也常常到地上来。他是天上的王，可是他也帮助住在地上的人们，关心[2]他们的生活和幸福。传说黄帝每次从天上下来的时候，是坐在一条龙的背上[3]。他来到地上时，常常住在东方的一个高山上。那时候，东方还没有国家，可是住在东方的人有很多很多。黄帝就帮助东方人开始了第一个国家，叫做中国。意思是说，这是黄帝住的国家。因为黄帝有东西南北四个脸，所以黄帝住的地方，永远是世界的中心。

　　传说黄帝经常帮助中国的人民，给他们幸福和平安的生活。可是黄帝给中国人的最大影响，是帮助他们开始国家和社会的生活。黄帝是一位很有能力的神，他身边[4]还有七十位有能力的神来帮助他。黄帝和他身边的神就帮助中国人，教他们用火[5]来烧饭吃。中国人会用火以後，就开始有了文化。

黄帝和他身边的神，还帮助了中国人许多的事情，教他们学会穿[6]衣服[7]。穿衣服也是文化的开始，因为穿上了衣服，人和动物就不一样了。黄帝还教了中国人很多的东西，他把音乐、医药[8]、和汉字带给了中国人。因为黄帝的帮助，东方就有了第一个国家。这就是今天的中国。

因为黄帝对中国人的帮助很大，影响了中国几千年的文化，所以中国人常常说自己是黄帝的後代[9]，他们觉得传说中的黄帝就是中国人的祖先[10]。因为传说中黄帝常常坐著龙走来走去，所以，中国人又喜欢用龙来表现中国的文化和历史上发生的事情。比如，中国人常常喜欢用龙来代表长城[11]和黄河[12]。

黄帝在世上的时候，天上的神和地上的人是可以随便来往[13]的。神到地上来和人到天上去都是很容易的。可是，传说後来黄帝回到天上去了。以後，天和地的路就不见了。天上的神就不容易再到地上来，地上的人也不容易到天上去了。

仓颉造字

仓颉是黄帝身边的一位神。他的工作是把每天发生的大事和小事都记下来，让人们可以知道和学习。可是那时候还没有发明文字[14]。仓颉记下来的事情没有一个人可以看懂。所以，仓颉就想办法，要发明一种文字。他希望用这种文字来记事[15]

和写历史，让後来的人可以知道以前发生过的事情。所以，仓颉每天就在想这件事情。

在远古的时候，中国人记事的方法，是在绳子上打结。每次发生什麼事情，就在绳子上打一个结。大事就打一个大结，小事就打一个小结。可是，这个记事的方法有一个麻烦。就是日子久了以後，虽然可以知道发生了多少事情，可是没有办法知道发生了什麼事情。

後来，有人就用画画的方法来记事。每一天发生的事情都画在木头[16]上或石头上，因为那时候还没有纸和笔。记在木头或石头上的事情比记在绳子上好多了。记事的人现在可以告诉别人过去发生了什麼事。看见这些画的人，大概也能猜出来过去发生了什麼事。

可是，画画也有很多的麻烦。因为在木头和石头上画画是很不容易的。而且，记下一件事情有的时候要画几个画。所以，记事情要花很多的时间，是一件很累人[17]的工作。有的时候，即使每天发生的事情并不重要，可是记事的工作却变成很重要。每天的事情也许并不忙，可是记事的人却变成了最忙的人了。

仓颉看见人们记事不容易，就天天想办法，要发明文字。他希望有了文字，人们记事会变得方便一些。後来的人也可以看得懂，以前古时候的人记下来的历史。所以，仓颉就天天想这件事情。有一天，仓颉看见了一只很大很大的乌龟[18]。这个乌龟年纪很大了，它的背上已经有了很多的花纹[19]，就像人老了，脸上有很多的皱纹[20]一样。

仓颉走近一看，看见有的花纹像山，有的花纹像水，又有的花纹像树。传说，仓颉有四只眼睛，所以看东西和别人不一样。仓颉这时想：为什麼不能用简单的线条[21]来代表要画的东西和事情呢？这样，记事就变得很容易了。如果能把这种用线条画画的方法，教给後来的人，大家就不都能看懂文字了吗？

仓颉就这样开始造起字来。他用最简单的线条来代表要画的东西的样子。这些就是最早的汉字，也叫"象形文字[22]"。仓颉造了多少个汉字呢？这个问题没有人能知道。後来的汉人又接著仓颉继续造字[23]。语言学家一般认为，现代[24]的汉字一共有六万多个，常用的汉字差不多有三千多个。有了汉字，中国文化就有了很大的变化。纸和笔也就发明出来了。汉字後来也流传[25]到了日本和东南亚[26]的一些国家。

阅读理解：

一、　黄帝为什麼是四个脸？

二、　黄帝给中国人最大的影响是什麼？

三、　中国人是怎样开始自己的文化的？

四、　为什麼说中国人是黄帝的後代？

五、　中国文化为什麼喜欢用龙来代表？

六、　仓颉的主要工作是什麼？

七、　古时候的人们用什麼方法来记事？

八、　仓颉是怎样发明文字的？

生字

1	黄帝	huángdì	the Yellow Emperor
2	关心	guānxīn	to be concerned about
3	背上	bèishàng	on the back
4	身边	shēnbiān	at his side
5	火	huǒ	fire
6	穿	chuān	to wear
7	衣服	yīfú	clothes
8	医药	yīyào	medicine
9	後代	hòudài	Posterity; later generations
10	祖先	zǔxiān	ancestors
11	长城	chángchéng	the Great Wall
12	黄河	huánghé	the Yellow River
13	来往	láiwǎng	to have contact
14	文字	wénzì	writing
15	记事	jìshì	to record
16	木头	mùtóu	wood
17	累人	lèirén	to be exhausting
18	乌龟	wūguī	tortoise
19	花纹	huāwén	pattern; design
20	皱纹	zhòuwén	wrinkles
21	线条	xiàntiáo	lines
22	象形文字	xiàngxíngwénzì	pictograph
23	造字	zàozì	to create words
24	现代	xiàndài	modern
25	流传	liúchuán	to spread; to hand down
26	东南亚	dōngnányǎ	Southeast Asia

Chapter 3   Yellow Emperor and Cang Jie Creates Written Words

The Yellow Emperor is not the emperor often mentioned in history. An emperor is the king of a country, the entire country belongs to him. The Yellow Emperor is a legendary god, the entire world belongs to him. He is the most important god in heaven: he is the king of all nature on earth, all animals, all mankind. Legend tells us that he has four faces that can see all directions: east, south, west, and north. That is why the Yellow Emperor knows about everything on heaven and earth.

The Yellow Emperor lives in heaven but he often comes down to earth. Although he is the king of heaven, he helps the people living on earth. He is concerned about their life and their happiness. According to legend, whenever the Yellow Emperor comes down to earth, he travels on the back of a dragon. When he comes to earth he often stays on a tall mountain in the east. In those days, there were no countries in the east, but there were many, many people living there. The Yellow Emperor helped the people in the east to start the first country, and it was called Middle Kingdom (China). This meant that it was the country where the Yellow Emperor lived. Because the Yellow Emperor had four faces facing east, west, south and north, the place where he lived would always be the center of the world.

Legend tells us that the Yellow Emperor frequently helped the people of China, he gave them a happy and peaceful life. However, the greatest thing he did for the Chinese people was to help them create a country and communal life. The Yellow Emperor is a god of great abilities, at his side are seventy other capable gods who assist him. The Yellow Emperor and the other gods helped the Chinese people. They taught them how to use fire and to cook food. When the Chinese people had learned how to use fire, their culture began to evolve.

The Yellow Emperor and his gods also helped the Chinese with other things. They taught the Chinese how to wear clothes. This, too, indicated the beginning of culture because clothes separated the people from the animals. The Yellow Emperor taught them many other things as well; he brought music, medicine, and writing to the Chinese people. Because of the Yellow Emperor's help, the east had the first country, and that is China. Because the Yellow Emperor's help was so very important and because he greatly influenced several thousand years of Chinese culture, the Chinese often say that they are his descendants, they believe that the legendary Yellow Emperor is their ancestor. The legendary Yellow Emperor often traveled on the back of a dragon, for this reason the Chinese often use the dragon to represent China's culture or history. An example of this is the dragon representing the Great Wall or the Yellow River.

When the Yellow Emperor was on earth, the gods in heaven and the people on earth could come and go as they pleased. It was easy for gods to come to earth or humans to go up to heaven. However, according to legend, the Emperor returned to heaven. After that the path between heaven and earth could no longer be seen. The gods in heaven could not come down to earth easily, and the people on earth could not return to heaven.

Cang Jie Creates Written Words

Cang Jie was one of the Yellow Emperor's serving gods. It was his job to remember all the important and less important things that happened each day so that people could know about them and learn from them. However, at that time, writing had not yet been invented. Nobody could understand what Cang Jie had recorded. Cang Jie spent time thinking about a way to develop writing. He hoped to use this writing to record things and to write down history so that their descendants would know what had happened in the past. Cang Jie spent every day thinking about this.

In archaic times, the Chinese people recorded things by tying knots in a rope. Every time something happened, a knot was tied into the rope. When something important happened, a big knot was tied; when something minor happened, a small knot was tied. However, this method had a drawback. After a certain period of time, even though we can tell that many things happened, we have no way of knowing what happened.

Later on, some people used drawings to record things. Pictures of daily occurrences were drawn on wood or rock because paper and paintbrushes didn't yet exist. Recording things on wood or stone was a lot better than remembering by tying knots in a rope. The people who recorded things could now tell others what had happened. Those who looked at the drawings could generally guess what had happened in the past.

However, the drawings had their difficulties as well. It was not easy to draw on wood or on stone; sometimes it took several drawings to describe one thing. Recording things took a lot of time and was a very tiring job. Sometimes the daily occurrences were not important at all, but by recording them, they became important. Sometimes a day was not busy at all, but by recording what happened, the person in charge of recording was very busy.

Cang Jie saw that the people were having a hard time recording things. Everyday he thought about finding a method, he wanted to discover writing. He hoped that writing would make the task of recording more convenient. Future generations would be able to understand ancient people's written history. Everyday Cang Jie thought about this problem. One day Cang Jie saw a very large tortoise. It was a very old tortoise, its back was covered with a pattern that looked like an old person with wrinkles all over his face.

Cang Jie approached the tortoise and noticed that some of its patterns looked like mountains, some looked like water, and some of the designs resembled trees. According to the legend, Cang Jie had four eyes and was able to see things differently from other people. He thought, why not use simple lines to represent the things and ideas we want to draw? Recording things would be much easier this way. If this method of drawing with lines can be taught to later generations, won't everybody be able to understand written words?

This is how Cang Jie started creating written words. He used the simplest lines to represent the shape of the things he wanted to draw. Those were the earliest Chinese characters, also called 'pictographs.' How many words did Cang Jie create? No one knows the answer to that question. Later generations followed Cang Jie and created more words. In general, philologists believe that there are more than 60,000

Chinese characters, more than 3,000 of which are commonly used. After writing was developed, Chinese culture changed a lot. Paper and paintbrushes were developed as well. Later on, Chinese characters also spread to Japan and some Southeast Asian countries.

第四章　孔子一生和老子思想

孔子一生

　　差不多在兩千多年前，中國出了一個很有名的人。他的名字叫孔子[1]。孔子是一個非常聰明的人，也是一個很有學問的人。那時，中國分成了很多個小國家。孔子就去這些小國家，見這些國家的國王，也見了很多重要的人。因為他是一個很有名的人，所以他們問了他很多的問題。對很多的問題，孔子都能提出自己很特別的看法。

孔子很小的時候，他的父母就去世[2]了。所以，家裏的生活不好，沒有很多錢用。可是，孔子是一個很有理想[3]的人。他希望別的國家接受[4]他的思想，也希望自己能為一個國王服務[5]。所以，孔子就從一個國家走到另一個國家，去和那些國家的國王見面。雖然有些國王喜歡他的思想，但卻沒有人接受他。

傳說，孔子有一次路過一個地方，遇見了一個七歲的孩子。這個小孩子在路的中間，造了一個小土城[6]，和其他的小朋友們在一起玩土城。這時，孔子的車子正好要從那條路上過去。孔子就下車來對那孩子說："你造的城正好在路上，我的車不能過去。你可以讓我們過去嗎？"小孩子回答說："從來沒有聽說城給車讓路的，只有聽說車走別的路經過城的。"

孔子見這個孩子很聰明，就問他幾個問題，想要看看他知道多少事情。沒想到那個小孩子都能回答出來。孔子就不再問他問題了。小孩子看見孔子不問了，就反問孔子一些問題，孔子卻沒有答出來，他很滿意那個小孩子的聰明。這個故事一直傳到今天，它告訴人們一個道理，孔子雖然是很有學問的人，可是他卻非常的和氣、謙虛[7]。

因為沒有人接受孔子的思想，所以孔子就收了許多的學生，開始教書。他希望把自己的思想教給他的學生。那時候，孔子的學生有三千個，其中有七十多個學生是非常好的學生。他寫了一部很有名的書，直到今天，這部書還是東方人和西方人在研究的一本很重要的書。

在這部書裏，孔子記下了他那個時代約兩百多年的歷史，也談了他對社會和國家的很多看法。他還告訴人們，在世界上應該怎樣生活。人和人應該怎樣來往。他的思想後來被整個中國文化和社會接受。孔子死了以後，他才成了中國古時候的大教育家[8]和大思想家[9]。

老子的故事

老子[10]和孔子是在同一個時代[11]，他們兩個人都是中國文化的祖先。但是，老子的傳說是比較奇怪的。老子一生的事情，被記在歷史書上的不多。即使是中國人，很多也不知道老子到底[12]是一個什麼樣的人。有些人還說，也許在歷史上並沒有老子這個人。但是，歷史上其實是有老子這個人的。

傳說老子在母親的肚子裏七十二年後才生下來。生下來的時候，他已經老了，頭髮[13]也白了。所以，母親給他一個名字叫老子。另外的一個傳說是，老子生下來就會說話，而且他的耳朵[14]很大，有差不多七尺[15]長。所以，他和平常人是不一樣的。

　　老子對中國文化的最大影響，是他寫的一本書，叫做“老子”。傳說，老子非常不滿意當時的社會和時代。他提出的思想是一個自然的人生。意思是，我們不應該故意地去使人生發生變化，而是用自然的方法去經歷人生。老子的思想是一個自然和安靜的人生。

　　老子因爲自己的思想不能被當時[16]的人們接受，就想要離開那個社會。結果，他坐上了牛車[17]，要到西方很遠很遠的地方去。但是，在路上他遇見了一個人。這個人非常希望向老子學習[18]，一定要老子住下來一些時候。他請老子把他自己的思想寫出來，留給後人[19]。老子沒有辦法，不得不答應。他就在主人的地方住了一些時候，寫出了一本五千字的書。這就是“老子”這本書。這本書直到今天還對東方和西方的思想有很大的影響。

閱讀理解：

一、　孔子是誰？

二、　談談孔子一生的兩、三個故事？

三、　孔子寫的一本書是什麼樣的書？

四、　爲什麼說老子也是中國文化的祖先？

五、　老子寫了一本什麼書？

六、　孔子的思想和老子的思想有什麼不同？

七、　談談你對孔子和老子思想的看法。

生字

¹ 孔子	kǒngzǐ	ㄎㄨㄥˇ ㄗˇ	*Confucius*
² 去世	qùshì	ㄑㄩˋ ㄕˋ	*to die*
³ 理想	lǐxiǎng	ㄌㄧˇ ㄒㄧㄤˇ	*ideal*
⁴ 接受	jiēshòu	ㄐㄧㄝ ㄕㄡˋ	*to accept*
⁵ 服務	fúwù	ㄈㄨˊ ㄨˋ	*to serve*
⁶ 土城	tǔchéng	ㄊㄨˇ ㄔㄥˊ	*a city made of clay*
⁷ 謙虛	qiānxū	ㄑㄧㄢ ㄒㄩ	*modest*
⁸ 教育家	jiāoyùjiā	ㄐㄧㄠ ㄩˋ ㄐㄧㄚ	*educator*
⁹ 思想家	sīxiǎngjiā	ㄙ ㄒㄧㄤˇ ㄐㄧㄚ	*philosopher*
¹⁰ 老子	lǎozǐ	ㄌㄠˇ ㄗˇ	*name of a philosopher*
¹¹ 時代	shídài	ㄕˊ ㄉㄞˋ	*generation*

[12] 到底	dàodǐ	ㄉㄠˋ ㄉㄧˇ	*after all*	
[13] 頭髮	tóufǎ	ㄊㄡˊ ㄈㄚˇ	*hair*	
[14] 耳朵	ěrduo	ㄦˇ ㄉㄨㄛˇ	*ear*	
[15] 尺	chǐ	ㄔˇ	*unit of length, 1/3 of a meter*	
[16] 當時	dāngshí	ㄉㄤ ㄕˊ	*of the time; at that time*	
[17] 牛車	niúchē	ㄋㄧㄡˊ ㄔㄜ	*oxcart*	
[18] 學習	xuéxí	ㄒㄩㄝˊ ㄒㄧˊ	*to study*	
[19] 後人	hòurén	ㄏㄡˋ ㄖㄣˊ	*later generations*	

第四章　孔子一生和老子思想

　　差不多在两千多年前，中国出了一个很有名的人。他的名字叫孔子[1]。孔子是一个非常聪明的人，也是一个很有学问的人。那时，中国分成了很多个小国家。孔子就去这些小国家，见这些国家的国王，也见了很多重要的人。因为他是一个很有名的人，所以他们问了他很多的问题。对很多的问题，孔子都能提出自己很特别的看法。

　　孔子很小的时候，他的父母就去世[2]了。所以，家里的生活不好，没有很多钱用。可是，孔子是一个很有理想[3]的人。他希望别的国家接受[4]他的思想，也希望自己能为一个国王服务[5]。所以，孔子就从一个国家走到另一个国家，去和那些国家的国王见面。虽然有些国王喜欢他的思想，但却没有人接受他。

　　传说，孔子有一次路过一个地方，遇见了一个七岁的孩子。这个小孩子在路的中间，造了一个小土城[6]，和其他的小朋友们在一起玩土城。这时，孔子的车子正好要从那条路上过去。孔子就下车来对那孩子说："你造的城正好在路上，我的车不能过去。你可以让我们过去吗？"小孩子回答说："从来没有听说城给车让路的，只有听说车走别的路经过城的。"

孔子见这个孩子很聪明，就问他几个问题，想要看看他知道多少事情。没想到那个小孩子都能回答出来。孔子就不再问他问题了。小孩子看见孔子不问了，就反问孔子一些问题，孔子却没有答出来，他很满意那个小孩子的聪明。这个故事一直传到今天，它告诉人们一个道理，孔子虽然是很有学问的人，可是他却非常的和气、谦虚[7]。

因为没有人接受孔子的思想，所以孔子就收了许多的学生，开始教书。他希望把自己的思想教给他的学生。那时候，孔子的学生有三千个，其中有七十多个学生是非常好的学生。他写了一部很有名的书，直到今天，这部书还是东方人和西方人在研究的一本很重要的书。

在这部书里，孔子记下了他那个时代约两百多年的历史，也谈了他对社会和国家的很多看法。他还告诉人们，在世界上应该怎样生活。人和人应该怎样来往。他的思想后来被整个中国文化和社会接受。孔子死了以后，他才成了中国古时候的大教育家[8]和大思想家[9]。

老子的故事

老子[10]和孔子是在同一个时代[11]，他们两个人都是中国文化的祖先。但是，老子的传说是比较奇怪的。老子一生的事情，被记在历史书上的不多。即使是中国人，很多也不知道老子到底[12]是一个什麼样的人。有些人还说，也许在历史上并没有老子这个人。但是，历史上其实是有老子这个人的。

传说老子在母亲的肚子里七十二年後才生下来。生下来的时候，他已经老了，头发[13]也白了。所以，母亲给他一个名字叫老子。另外的一个传说是，老子生下来就会说话，而且他的耳朵[14]很大，有差不多七尺[15]长。所以，他和平常人是不一样的。

老子对中国文化的最大影响，是他写的一本书，叫做"老子"。传说，老子非常不满意当时的社会和时代。他提出的思想是一个自然的人生。意思是，我们不应该故意地去使人生发生变化，而是用自然的方法去经历人生。老子的思想是一个自然和安静的人生。

老子因为自己的思想不能被当时[16]的人们接受，就想要离开那个社会。结果，他坐上了牛车[17]，要到西方很远很远的地方去。但是，在路上他遇见了一个人。这个人非常希望向老子学习[18]，一定要老子住下来一些时候。他请老子把他自己的思想写出来，留给後人[19]。老子没有办法，不得不答应。他就在主人的地方住了一些时候，写出了一本五千字的书。这就是"老子"这本书。这本书直到今天还对东方和西方的思想有很大的影响。

阅读理解：

一、 孔子是谁？

二、 谈谈孔子一生的两、三个故事？

三、 孔子写的一本书是什麽样的书？

四、 为什麽说老子也是中国文化的祖先？

五、 老子写了一本什麽书？

六、 孔子的思想和老子的思想有什麽不同？

七、 谈谈你对孔子和老子思想的看法。

生字

1	孔子	kǒngzǐ	Confucius
2	去世	qùshì	to die
3	理想	lǐxiǎng	ideal
4	接受	jiēshòu	to accept
5	服务	fúwù	to serve
6	土城	tǔchéng	a city made of clay
7	谦虚	qiānxū	modest
8	教育家	jiāoyùjiā	educator
9	思想家	sīxiǎngjiā	philosopher
10	老子	lǎozǐ	name of a philosopher
11	时代	shídài	generation
12	到底	dàodǐ	after all
13	头发	tóufā	hair
14	耳朵	ěrduo	ear
15	尺	chǐ	unit of length, 1/3 of a meter
16	当时	dāngshí	of the time; at that time
17	牛车	niúchē	oxcart
18	学习	xuéxí	to study
19	後人	hòurén	later generations

Chapter 4   The Life of Confucius and the Philosophy of Lao Tzu

About two thousand years ago, a very famous man appeared in China. His name was Confucius. Confucius was a very intelligent man, he was also a man of great learning. At that time, China was made up of many small countries. Confucius went to these small countries and visited their kings and many other important people. Because he was such a famous man, they all asked him questions. Confucius had a very personal and particular approach to these questions.

Confucius' parents died when he was very young. His life at home was difficult and there wasn't much money around. But Confucius was idealistic, he hoped that one of the countries would accept his philosophy and that he himself would be able to serve a king. Therefore, Confucius went from country to country to talk to kings in those countries. While many kings were interested in Confucius' ideas, none of them would accept his ideas.

It is said that one day when Confucius was passing through a town, he came across a seven-year-old boy. This little boy was in the middle of the road where he had built a clay city, and he and his friends were playing with the city. The wagon which Confucius was riding in wanted to take that same road, so Confucius got down from the wagon and said to the boy, "The city that you have built is in the middle of the road, my wagon cannot get by. Would you mind letting us get by?" The young boy answered, "I have never heard of a city giving way to a wagon, I've only heard of wagons taking a different route to get through the city."

Confucius could see that the boy was very clever, so he asked him some questions to test the boy's knowledge. He hadn't imagined that the boy would be able to answer all of his questions, and when the boy did, Confucius stopped his questioning. When the boy realized that Confucius was not asking any more questions, the boy started asking questions himself. When Confucius wasn't able to answer all the questions, he was convinced of the boy's intelligence. This story is still being told today because it tells us a basic truth: Although Confucius was a man of great learning, he was also very kind and very modest.

Because the kings weren't interested in Confucius' philosophy, he took on a group of students and began to teach them. He hoped to teach his ideas to his students. At one time, Confucius had 3,000 students, among them were about seventy students who were exceptional.

Confucius also wrote a famous book which people in the East and West still study today. In this book, Confucius recorded about 200 years of the history of his time, he also described his opinion of society and of his country. He also tells us how to live in this world and how people should interact with each other. Later on, his philosophy became part of Chinese culture and society. It was not until after his death that he was considered one of China's great educators and philosophers.

The Story of Lao Tzu

Lao Tzu and Confucius lived during the same period. They are the forefathers of Chinese culture. However, Lao Tzu's legend is rather unusual. There is very little written about Lao Tzu's life in the history books. Even among Chinese, there are many who don't really know what kind of a person he was. Some people even say that Lao Tzu never actually existed. Historical fact, however, tells us that there was such a man.

According to the legend, Lao Tzu stayed inside his mother's womb for seventy-two years before he was born. He was already an old man with white hair when he was born. That is why his mother called him Old Child (Lao Tzu). Another legend claims that he could talk as soon as he was born and that his ears were very big; in fact, his ears were said to be about seven chi long. He was not like other ordinary people.

Lao Tzu's greatest influence on Chinese culture is the book he wrote called Lao Tzu. It is said that Lao Tzu was not at all happy with the contemporary society and generation. He put forward the concept of life following its natural course. He believed that we should not purposefully try to change life, life should be experienced according to its natural course. According to Lao Tzu, life should be lived in accordance with nature and in tranquillity.

Because the people of that time could not accept Lao Tzu's philosophy, he wanted to leave that society. He got onto an ox cart with the intention of traveling far to the west. Along the way, however, he met a man who very much wanted to learn from him, and the man convinced Lao Tzu to stay for awhile. The man asked Lao Tzu to write down his thoughts so that they could be kept for later generations. Lao Tzu had no choice, he could not refuse. He stayed with his host for a certain time and wrote his 5,000-word book called Lao Tzu. Even today, this book has a great influence on both eastern and western philosophy.

第五章　　秦始皇帝和末代皇帝

秦始皇

　　中國的歷史很長很長，用文字記下來的歷史，就有二千五百年左右。沒有用文字記下來的歷史，差不多也有二千五百年那麼長。所以，人們說中國有五千年的歷史是不錯的。中國是世界上最古老的國家之一。在這麼長的歷史裏，中國一共經過了二十多個朝代[1]。其中最長的朝代有八百多年的歷史，最短的朝代只有十五年的時間。中國歷史上的第一個皇帝，就是出在最短的那個朝代裏。

皇帝和國王不一樣。皇帝是整個中國的王，國王卻只是在中國裏面的小國家的王。在中國歷史上，有時候，整個中國分成了幾個小的國家。這時候，每一個國家都有自己的國王。當中國又變成了一個國家，那時，中國就會有一個皇帝。當然，這時候皇帝的手下[2]，還是有不同地方的王，可是這已經不是一個國家的王了。

中國歷史上記下來的第一個皇帝是秦[3]始[4]皇。秦始皇[5]在當皇帝以前，也是一個小國家的國王，這個國家叫秦國[6]。後來秦國的國王打下[7]了當時的其它六個小國家，統一[8]了全中國。結果，他就成了中國歷史上的第一個皇帝，叫秦始皇。因爲他是中國有文字歷史以來的第一個皇帝，也就是說，皇帝的歷史是從他開始的。

秦始皇打下了天下以後，就開始統一國家的文字和錢幣[9]。他又建造[10]了很多的公路[11]，後來又用了七十萬人來建他的皇宮[12]、墳墓[13]和長城。這些建造的工作，使很多人最後都累死了。因爲這樣，歷史上很多的人，都認爲秦始皇是一個很壞[14]的皇帝。

歷史告訴我們，秦始皇作了皇帝以後，對當時的人民非常[15]不好，他作了一些很壞的事情。其中經常被人談起的事情是，秦始皇燒了全國的書，又殺[16]了幾萬個讀書人[17]。他這樣做是爲了不讓別人知道，以前的歷史和世界上發生的事。這樣，他就可以永遠作皇帝。

可是，他這樣作的結果，卻是使千千萬萬的人起來反對他，所以後來秦始皇的國家和朝代很快就沒有了。他雖然二十一歲就作了皇帝，他死的時候只有五十歲。中國人常常把喜歡殺人的皇帝比作[18]秦始皇，因爲秦始皇把自己的父親都殺了。

末代[19]皇帝

中國經過了二十多個朝代，一共兩千多年，最後才開始接受現代西方文化的影響。中國最後的一個朝代是清朝[20]，到了清朝的時候，中國已經像是一個很老很老的老頭子[21]了。這時，中國最需要的是社會和文化的變化。

清朝在中國有三百年的歷史，它的最後一個皇帝是溥儀[22]，他也是中國歷史上最後的一個皇帝。那時候，中國社會已經發生了很大的變化，西方的科技[23]和文化思想已經開始影響中國人的生活，如汽車，火車[24]，工廠，大學，和醫院[25]等。但是，這種變化是非常不容易的，因爲幾千年來，中國人是不喜歡變化的。

溥儀作皇帝的時候，才只有三歲，那是一九〇九年。他作皇帝以後，就在皇宮裏，一直到長大。在皇宮裏，他有四個媽媽。可是，真正養他長大的是他的奶媽[26]，是花錢[27]從皇宮外請來的。他的一生，別人都把他看作是皇帝。其實他一點自由[28]也沒有，沒有真正[29]的朋友，也不能離開皇宮。他直到一九六二年才真正結婚，那時候他已經五十多歲了。他的太太是北京的一位護士[30]，結婚後，溥儀過了五年的家庭[31]生活。

溥儀的一生非常特別，從小到大經過了五個政治[32]變化的時期[33]。最後，當他得到自由的時候，他很快就死去了。

閱讀理解：

一、　中國的歷史有多長？

二、　中國的歷中最長的朝代有多久？最短的朝代呢？

三、　中國歷史上第一個皇帝是怎樣來的？

四、　秦始皇在歷史上做了什麼大事？

五、　秦始皇在歷史上做了那些壞事？

六、　溥儀的一生為麼很特別？

七、　中國歷史上的朝代是怎樣結束的？

八、　談談你對中國歷史上朝代的看法。

生字

1	朝代	cháodài	ㄔㄠˊ ㄉㄞˋ	dynasty
2	手下	shǒuxià	ㄕㄡˇ ㄒㄧㄚˋ	under the leadership; under
3	秦	qín	ㄑㄧㄣˊ	relating to the Qin; a surname
4	始	shǐ	ㄕˇ	to start
5	秦始皇	qínshǐhuáng	ㄑㄧㄣˊ ㄕˇ ㄏㄨㄤˊ	the first emperor of China
6	秦國	qínguó	ㄑㄧㄣˊ ㄍㄨㄛˊ	the kingdom of Qin
7	打下	dǎxià	ㄉㄚˇ ㄒㄧㄚˋ	to conquer
8	統一	tǒngyī	ㄊㄨㄥˇ ㄧ	to unite; to unify
9	錢幣	qiánbì	ㄑㄧㄢˊ ㄅㄧˋ	coin; money
10	建造	jiànzào	ㄐㄧㄢˋ ㄗㄠˋ	to build
11	公路	gōnglù	ㄍㄨㄥ ㄌㄨˋ	road
12	皇宮	huánggōng	ㄏㄨㄤˊ ㄍㄨㄥ	imperial palace
13	墳墓	fénmù	ㄈㄣˊ ㄇㄨˋ	grave; tomb
14	壞	huài	ㄏㄨㄞˋ	bad; evil
15	非常	fēicháng	ㄈㄟ ㄔㄤˊ	very
16	殺	shā	ㄕㄚ	to kill
17	讀書人	dúshūrén	ㄉㄨˊ ㄕㄨ ㄖㄣˊ	intellectuals
18	比作	bǐzuò	ㄅㄧˇ ㄗㄨㄛˋ	to describe...as
19	末代	mòdài	ㄇㄛˋ ㄉㄞˋ	the last reign of a dynasty
20	清朝	qīngcháo	ㄑㄧㄥ ㄔㄠˊ	the Qing Dynasty
21	老頭子	lǎotóuzi	ㄌㄠˇ ㄊㄡˊ ㄗ˙	old man
22	溥儀	pǔyí	ㄆㄨˇ ㄧˊ	name of the last emperor of China

²³ 科技	kējì	ㄎㄜ ㄐㄧˋ	*science and technology*
²⁴ 火車	huǒchē	ㄏㄨㄛˇ ㄔㄜ	*train*
²⁵ 醫院	yīyuàn	ㄧ ㄩㄢˋ	*hospital*
²⁶ 奶媽	nǎimā	ㄋㄞˇ ㄇㄚ	*wet nurse*
²⁷ 花錢	huāqián	ㄏㄨㄚ ㄑㄧㄢˊ	*to spend money*
²⁸ 自由	zìyóu	ㄗˋ ㄧㄡˊ	*freedom*
²⁹ 真正	zhēnzhèng	ㄓㄣ ㄓㄥˋ	*real; properly*
³⁰ 護士	hùshì	ㄏㄨˋ ㄕˋ	*nurse*
³¹ 家庭	jiātíng	ㄐㄧㄚ ㄊㄧㄥˊ	*family*
³² 政治	zhèngzhì	ㄓㄥˋ ㄓˋ	*politics; political*
³³ 時期	shíqi	ㄕˊ ㄑㄧˊ	*time period*

第五章　　秦始皇帝和末代皇帝

中国的历史很长很长，用文字记下来的历史，就有二千五百年左右。没有用文字记下来的历史，差不多也有二千五百年那麼长。所以，人们说中国有五千年的历史是不错的。中国是世界上最古老的国家之一。在这麼长的历史里，中国一共经过了二十多个朝代[1]。其中最长的朝代有八百多年的历史，最短的朝代只有十五年的时间。中国历史上的第一个皇帝，就是出在最短的那个朝代里。

皇帝和国王不一样。皇帝是整个中国的王，国王却只是在中国里面的小国家的王。在中国历史上，有时候，整个中国分成了几个小的国家。这时候，每一个国家都有自己的国王。当中国又变成了一个国家，那时，中国就会有一个皇帝。当然，这时候皇帝的手下[2]，还是有不同地方的王，可是这已经不是一个国家的王了。

中国历史上记下来的第一个皇帝是秦[3]始[4]皇。秦始皇[5]在当皇帝以前，也是一个小国家的国王，这个国家叫秦国[6]。後来秦国的国王打下[7]了当时的其它六个小国家，统一[8]了全中国。

结果，他就成了中国历史上的第一个皇帝，叫秦始皇。因为他是中国有文字历史以来的第一个皇帝，也就是说，皇帝的历史是从他开始的。

秦始皇打下了天下以後，就开始统一国家的文字和钱币[9]。他又建造[10]了很多的公路[11]，後来又用了七十万人来建他的皇宫[12]、坟墓[13]和长城。这些建造的工作，使很多人最後都累死了。因为这样，历史上很多的人，都认为秦始皇是一个很坏[14]的皇帝。

历史告诉我们，秦始皇作了皇帝以後，对当时的人民非常[15]不好，他作了一些很坏的事情。其中经常被人谈起的事情是，秦始皇烧了全国的书，又杀[16]了几万个读书人[17]。他这样做是为了不让别人知道，以前的历史和世界上发生的事。这样，他就可以永远作皇帝。

可是，他这样作的结果，却是使千千万万的人起来反对他，所以後来秦始皇的国家和朝代很快就没有了。他虽然二十一岁就作了皇帝，他死的时候只有五十岁。中国人常常把喜欢杀人的皇帝比作[18]秦始皇，因为秦始皇把自己的父亲都杀了。

末代[19]皇帝

中国经过了二十多个朝代，一共两千多年，最後才开始接受现代西方文化的影响。中国最後的一个朝代是清朝[20]，到了清朝的时候，中国已经像是一个很老很老的老头子[21]了。这时，中国最需要的是社会和文化的变化。

清朝在中国有三百年的历史，它的最後一个皇帝是溥仪[22]，他也是中国历史上最後的一个皇帝。那时候，中国社会已经发生了很大的变化，西方的科技[23]和文化思想已经开始影响中国人的生活，如汽车，火车[24]，工厂，大学，和医院[25]等。但是，这种变化是非常不容易的，因为几千年来，中国人是不喜欢变化的。

溥仪作皇帝的时候，才只有三岁，那是一九〇九年。他作皇帝以後，就在皇宫里，一直到长大。在皇宫里，他有四个妈妈。可是，真正养他长大的是他的奶妈[26]，是花钱[27]从皇宫外请来的。他的一生，别人都把他看作是皇帝。其实他一点自由[28]也没有，没有真正[29]的朋友，也不能离开皇宫。他直到一九六二年才真正结婚，那时候他已经五十多岁了。他的太太是北京的一位护士[30]，结婚後，溥仪过了五年的家庭[31]生活。

溥仪的一生非常特别，从小到大经过了五个政治[32]变化的时期[33]。最後，当他得到自由的时候，他很快就死去了。

阅读理解：

一、　中国的历史有多长？

二、　中国的历中最长的朝代有多久？最短的朝代呢？

三、　中国历史上第一个皇帝是怎样来的？

四、　秦始皇在历史上做了什麽大事？

五、　秦始皇在历史上做了那些坏事？

六、　溥仪的一生为麽很特别？

七、　中国历史上的朝代是怎样结束的？

八、　谈谈你对中国历史上朝代的看法。

生字

1	朝代	cháodài	dynasty
2	手下	shǒuxià	under the leadership; under
3	秦	qín	relating to the Qin; a surname
4	始	shǐ	to start
5	秦始皇	qínshǐhuáng	the first emperor of China
6	秦国	qínguó	the kingdom of Qin
7	打下	dǎxià	to conquer
8	统一	tǒngyī	to unite; to unify
9	钱币	qiánbì	coin; money

10	建造	jiànzào	to build
11	公路	gōnglù	road
12	皇宫	huánggōng	imperial palace
13	坟墓	fénmù	grave; tomb
14	坏	huài	bad; evil
15	非常	fēicháng	very
16	杀	shā	to kill
17	读书人	dúshūrén	intellectuals
18	比作	bǐzuò	to describe...as
19	末代	mòdài	the last reign of a dynasty
20	清朝	qīngcháo	the Qing Dynasty
21	老头子	lǎotóuzi	old man
22	溥仪	pǔyí	name of the last emperor of China
23	科技	kējì	science and technology
24	火车	huǒchē	train
25	医院	yīyuàn	hospital
26	奶妈	nǎimā	wet nurse
27	花钱	huāqián	to spend money
28	自由	zìyóu	freedom
29	真正	zhēnzhèng	real; properly
30	护士	hùshì	nurse
31	家庭	jiātíng	family
32	政治	zhèngzhì	politics; political
33	时期	shíqī	time period

Chapter 5   The First Emperor Qin Shi Huang and the Last Emperor of a Dynasty

The history of China is extremely long; the written history is about 2,500-years-old. Before writing was used to record events, there were also about 2,500 years of unwritten history. It is therefore not wrong to say that China has a 5,000-year-history. China is one of the oldest countries in the world. There were more than twenty dynasties in China during this long history. The longest dynasty lasted over 800 years, the shortest lasted only fifteen years. The first emperor of China lived during that short dynasty.

Emperors and kings were not the same. The emperor was the king of all of China; a king was the king of a small country within China. At certain times during China's history, the country was divided up into several smaller countries. At that time, each country had its own king. At the time when China was unified into one country, it had an emperor. Of course there were still kings who were subservient to the emperor, but they were no longer like the previous kings of the smaller countries.

The first historically recorded emperor was Qin Shi Huang. Before he became emperor, he had been the king of a small country called Qin. The king of the country of Qin defeated the other seven countries and united China. As a result, he became the first emperor in China's history and was called Qin Shi Huang. Because he is the first emperor in written history, we can say that imperial history started with him.

After Qin Shi Huang's victory, he standardized the countries' writing and money. Later on, he also built many roads and used 700,000 people to build his palace, his tomb, and the Great Wall. Many people ended up dying because of these construction projects. For this reason (and many other reasons as well), throughout history, many people have considered Qin Shi Huang to be an extremely cruel emperor.

History tells us that after Qin Shi Huang became emperor, he was very cruel to the people. He did several evil things. One of the most frequently mentioned is that he burned all the books in the country and had many thousands of scholars killed. He did this because he didn't want people to know about past history or the events of the world. He hoped that in this way he would be emperor forever.

However, the result of his actions was that millions and millions of people ended up opposing him, and his dynasty soon came to an end. Although he became emperor when he was twenty-one, he died when he was only fifty-years-old. Emperors who enjoyed killing people were often compared to Qin Shi Huang because Qin Shi Huang had his own father killed.

The Last Emperor of a Dynasty

In over 2,000 years, China went through more than twenty dynasties until it finally began to be influenced by modern western culture. The last Chinese dynasty was the Qing Dynasty. During the Qing Dynasty,

China already resembled an ancient old man. China was in great need of societal and cultural change.

The Qing Dynasty lasted about 300 years and its last emperor was called Pu Yi. He was also the last emperor of China. At that time, China had already undergone significant changes. Western science and technology and cultural concepts such as cars, trains, factories, universities, hospitals, etc. had already started to be introduced into Chinese life. These changes did not come easily, however, because the Chinese had been opposed to change for several thousand years.

When Pu Yi became emperor, he was only three-years-old, that was in 1909. After he became emperor, he spent all his time inside the Imperial Palace until he was an adult. Inside the palace he had four mothers. The one who actually raised him was a wet nurse who had been hired from outside the palace. During his entire life, people treated him differently because he was the emperor. But he had no real freedom. He had no real friends and the imperial officials wouldn't allow him to leave the palace. He didn't get properly married until 1962 when he was already fifty-years-old. His wife was a nurse from Beijing. After getting married, Pu Yi spent five years living a family life at home.

Pu Yi had a very unusual life. During his life he witnessed five periods of political change. In the end, when officials finally granted him his freedom, he passed away quite soon thereafter.

第六章　　管仲得友和堯舜皇帝

管仲得友

堯舜皇帝

　　古時候，有兩個好朋友，一個名字叫管仲[1]，另一個名字叫鮑叔牙[2]。他們倆從小就在一起長大，一起玩。他們的故事發生在兩千多年前的中國。因爲這個故事非常特別，所以雖然過了兩千多年，人們還是喜歡把它傳給後人。它告訴人們一個道理，就是什麼是真正的朋友。

　　鮑叔牙比管仲有錢。他們有一個時候在一起做生意。生意做成了，管仲總是多分一些錢。別的朋友看見了不明白，也不高興。他們說："做生意用的是鮑叔牙的錢，爲什麼管仲要多分一些？"鮑叔牙卻說："他家裏的生活不好，應該多拿一些錢。因爲他有一個老母親，很需要錢用。"

　　年輕的時候，鮑叔牙和管仲一起去打仗[3]。打仗的時候，鮑叔牙總是[4]跑在前面，管仲總是跟在鮑叔牙的後面。大家都說，管仲很怕死。鮑叔牙卻說，管仲不是怕死，而是小心。因爲他家裏有老人需要他，如果他不小心死了，那真是太可惜了。

　　後來，管仲希望爲別人工作。他幾次得到了工作的機會又做不下去，就離開了。別人都說管仲無用[5]，什麼事都做不好。鮑叔牙卻說，管仲不是沒有用，而是沒有遇見真正認識他的人。因爲管仲其實是一位很有才能的人，只是他的機會還沒有到。

　　最後，鮑叔牙把管仲介紹給了一個國王。國王聽了鮑叔牙的話，就重用[6]了管仲。結果，管仲就爲國王服務，使這個國家發生了重大[7]的變化，成了一個大國。管仲非常感謝鮑叔牙的幫助。他說："生我、養[8]我的是我的父母，可是真正認識我，幫助我的是鮑叔牙。他是我真正的朋友！"

堯[9]舜皇帝

　　上古的時候，傳說有一個非常好的皇帝，名叫堯。堯在中國歷史上是很出名的，因爲他的心很好，給了人民的生活很大的幸福。他從不隨便花[10]國家和人民的錢，而且花很大的力氣工作，來幫助國家和人民。所以，他作皇帝的時候，人民非常滿意，國家也十分平安。傳說這是中國歷史上最好的時期之一[11]。

　　堯有十個兒子，但是他的大兒子從小就很不聽話[12]。大兒子不喜歡讀書，只喜歡玩。而且，他對人非常不好，不像他的爸爸。堯爲了這個孩子心裏很著急[13]，想了各種的方法要給他好的影響。所以，堯發明了"圍棋[14]"，讓大兒子玩。堯希望用圍棋來教大兒子學一些東西。可是，大兒子玩了一些時候，就沒有興趣了。

　　在中國古的時候，只有皇帝的兒子才可以作皇帝，別人是不可以的。堯看見大兒子這麼不聽話，也不學習。他心裏知道，大兒子是不能作皇帝的。如果大兒子作了皇帝，天下一定會變得非常的糟糕。所以，堯就不想讓大兒子作皇帝，也不想讓自己其他的兒子作皇帝。他希望能找到一個真正有才能和有好名聲的人。這樣，當堯年紀老的時候，他就可以休息，讓別人來作皇帝。

　　結果，堯找到了一個人。這個人名叫舜。舜生在一個很平常的農民[15]家庭。他從小就很會做事。他也很會種田和打魚[16]，還會造很多的東西。堯見了舜，就很喜歡他，想要讓舜接下去[17]作皇帝。可是，舜覺得自己不是皇帝的兒子，不應該去作皇帝。堯因爲舜不自私[18]，就更喜歡舜。他就把自己的兩個女兒嫁[19]給了舜。

堯的大兒子聽說父親要把皇帝給別人作，很生氣。他就起來反對父親，要和父親打仗。結果，堯真的和兒子打起仗來了。大兒子看打不過[20]父親，也知道自己做的事情是錯的，就在大海的邊上自殺[21]了。舜就作了皇帝。堯讓舜作皇帝的故事，一直流傳[22]到了今天。

閱讀理解：

一、 鮑叔牙是怎樣幫助管仲的？

二、 管仲後來怎麼樣？

三、 中國人希望的皇帝是什麼樣的皇帝？

四、 中國歷史上的一個朝代是怎樣繼續下去的？

五、 舜作皇帝爲什麼很特別？

六、 爲什麼說堯是一個很好的皇帝？

七、 談談你對中國皇帝的認識？你知道有那些好皇帝嗎？

生字

1	管仲	guǎnzhòng	ㄍㄨㄢˇ ㄓㄨㄥˋ	*name of the person in this story*
2	鮑叔牙	bàoshúyá	ㄅㄠˋ ㄕㄨˊ ㄧㄚˊ	*Guan Zhong's friend*
3	打仗	dǎzhàng	ㄉㄚˇ ㄓㄤˋ	*war*
4	總是	zǒngshì	ㄗㄨㄥˇ ㄕˋ	*always*
5	無用	wúyòng	ㄨˊ ㄩㄥˋ	*useless*
6	重用	zhòngyòng	ㄓㄨㄥˋ ㄩㄥˋ	*to put someone in an important position*
7	重大	zhòngdà	ㄓㄨㄥˋ ㄉㄚˋ	*great*
8	養	yǎng	ㄧㄤˇ	*to raise*
9	堯	yáo	ㄧㄠˊ	*name of a legendary emperor*
10	花	huā	ㄏㄨㄚ	*to spend*
11	之一	zhīyī	ㄓ ㄧ	*one of*
12	聽話	tīnghuà	ㄊㄧㄥ ㄏㄨㄚˋ	*obedient*
13	著急	zhāojí	ㄓㄠ ㄐㄧˊ	*nervous; worried*
14	圍棋	wéiqí	ㄨㄟˊ ㄑㄧˊ	*a Chinese board game played with black and white pieces; Go*
15	農民	nóngmín	ㄋㄨㄥˊ ㄇㄧㄣˊ	*peasant*
16	打魚	dǎyú	ㄉㄚˇ ㄩˊ	*to fish*
17	接下去	jiēxiàqù	ㄐㄧㄝ ㄒㄧㄚˋ ㄑㄩˋ	*to follow*
18	自私	zìsī	ㄗˋ ㄙ	*selfish*
19	嫁	jià	ㄐㄧㄚˋ	*to marry off*
20	打不過	dǎbùguò	ㄉㄚˇ ㄅㄨˋ ㄍㄨㄛˋ	*cannot defeat*
21	自殺	zìshā	ㄗˋ ㄕㄚ	*to commit suicide*
22	流傳	liúchuán	ㄌㄧㄡˊ ㄔㄨㄢˊ	*to pass down; to hand down*

第六章　　　管仲得友和尧舜皇帝

古时候，有两个好朋友，一个名字叫管仲[1]，另一个名字叫鲍叔牙[2]。他们俩从小就在一起长大，一起玩。他们的故事发生在两千多年前的中国。因为这个故事非常特别，所以虽然过了两千多年，人们还是喜欢把它传给後人。它告诉人们一个道理，就是什麼是真正的朋友。

鲍叔牙比管仲有钱。他们有一个时候在一起做生意。生意做成了，管仲总是多分一些钱。别的朋友看见了不明白，也不高兴。他们说："做生意用的是鲍叔牙的钱，为什麼管仲要多分一些？"鲍叔牙却说："他家里的生活不好，应该多拿一些钱。因为他有一个老母亲，很需要钱用。"

年轻的时候，鲍叔牙和管仲一起去打仗[3]。打仗的时候，鲍叔牙总是[4]跑在前面，管仲总是跟在鲍叔牙的後面。大家都说，管仲很怕死。鲍叔牙却说，管仲不是怕死，而是小心。因为他家里有老人需要他，如果他不小心死了，那真是太可惜了。

後来，管仲希望为别人工作。他几次得到了工作的机会又做不下去，就离开了。别人都说管仲无用[5]，什麼事都做不好。

鲍叔牙却说，管仲不是没有用，而是没有遇见真正认识他的人。因为管仲其实是一位很有才能的人，只是他的机会还没有到。

最後，鲍叔牙把管仲介绍给了一个国王。国王听了鲍叔牙的话，就重用[6]了管仲。结果，管仲就为国王服务，使这个国家发生了重大[7]的变化，成了一个大国。管仲非常感谢鲍叔牙的帮助。他说："生我、养[8]我的是我的父母，可是真正认识我，帮助我的是鲍叔牙。他是我真正的朋友！"

尧[9]舜皇帝

上古的时候，传说有一个非常好的皇帝，名叫尧。尧在中国历史上是很出名的，因为他的心很好，给了人民的生活很大的幸福。他从不随便花[10]国家和人民的钱，而且花很大的力气工作，来帮助国家和人民。所以，他作皇帝的时候，人民非常满意，国家也十分平安。传说这是中国历史上最好的时期之一[11]。

尧有十个儿子，但是他的大儿子从小就很不听话[12]。大儿子不喜欢读书，只喜欢玩。而且，他对人非常不好，不像他的爸爸。尧为了这个孩子心里很著急[13]，想了各种的方法要给他好的影响。所以，尧发明了"围棋[14]"，让大儿子玩。尧希望用围棋来教大儿子学一些东西。可是，大儿子玩了一些时候，就没有兴趣了。

在中国古的时候，只有皇帝的儿子才可以作皇帝，别人是不可以的。尧看见大儿子这麽不听话，也不学习。他心里知道，大儿子是不能作皇帝的。如果大儿子作了皇帝，天下一定会变得非常的糟糕。所以，尧就不想让大儿子作皇帝，也不想让自己其他的儿子作皇帝。他希望能找到一个真正有才能和有好名声的人。这样，当尧年纪老的时候，他就可以休息，让别人来作皇帝。

结果，尧找到了一个人。这个人名叫舜。舜生在一个很平常的农民[15]家庭。他从小就很会做事。他也很会种田和打鱼[16]，还会造很多的东西。尧见了舜，就很喜欢他，想要让舜接下去[17]作皇帝。可是，舜觉得自己不是皇帝的儿子，不应该去作皇帝。尧因为舜不自私[18]，就更喜欢舜。他就把自己的两个女儿嫁[19]给了舜。

尧的大儿子听说父亲要把皇帝给别人作，很生气。他就起来反对父亲，要和父亲打仗。结果，尧真的和儿子打起仗来了。大儿子看打不过[20]父亲，也知道自己做的事情是错的，就在大海的边上自杀[21]了。舜就作了皇帝。尧让舜作皇帝的故事，一直流传[22]到了今天。

阅读理解：

一、　鲍叔牙是怎样帮助管仲的？

二、　管仲後来怎麼样？

三、　中国人希望的皇帝是什麼样的皇帝？

四、　中国历史上的一个朝代是怎样继续下去的？

五、　舜作皇帝为什麼很特别？

六、　为什麼说尧是一个很好的皇帝？

七、　谈谈你对中国皇帝的认识？你知道有那些好皇帝吗？

生字

1	管仲	guǎnzhòng	name of the person in this story
2	鲍叔牙	bàoshúyá	Guan Zhong's friend
3	打仗	dǎzhàng	war
4	总是	zǒngshì	always
5	无用	wúyòng	useless
6	重用	zhòngyòng	to put someone in an important position
7	重大	zhòngdà	great
8	养	yǎng	to raise
9	尧	yáo	name of a legendary emperor
10	花	huā	to spend
11	之一	zhīyī	one of
12	听话	tīnghuà	obedient
13	著急	zháojí	nervous; worried
14	围棋	wéiqí	a Chinese board game played with black and white pieces; Go
15	农民	nóngmín	peasant
16	打鱼	dǎyú	to fish
17	接下去	jiēxiàqù	to follow
18	自私	zìsī	selfish
19	嫁	jià	to marry off
20	打不过	dǎbùguò	cannot defeat
21	自杀	zìshā	to commit suicide
22	流传	liúchuán	to pass down; to hand down

Chapter 6　Guan Zhong Finds Friendship and the Emperors Yao and Shun

In ancient times, there were two good friends, one was called Guan Zhong and the other was called Bao Shu Ya. The two had been together since childhood: they grew up together and played together. This story happened in China over 2,000 years ago. It is an exceptional story and even though it is over 2,000 years old, people still like to pass it on to the next generation. The story teaches us a basic truth about friendship.

Bao Shu Ya was richer than Guan Zhong. At one point they ran businesses together. After each business deal, Guan Zhong always took a little more than his share. Other friends saw this and didn't understand, they didn't like it. They said, "The business was started with Bao Shu Ya's money, why is it that Guan Zhong takes more than his share?" Bao Shu Ya, however, explained, "His family doesn't have an easy life, he needs to take a little more money. He has an old mother, he needs more money."

In their youth, Bao Shu Ya and Guan Zhong went to war together. Bao Shu Ya always ran up to the front, but Guan Zhong always followed and stayed behind Bao Shu Ya. Everybody claimed that Guan Zhong was afraid to die, but Bao Shu Ya countered, "Guan Zhong is not afraid of dying, he is simply being careful. The old people in his home need him and if he isn't careful and dies, it would be a terrible shame."

Later on, Guan Zhong wanted to go work for someone. Every time he was offered a job, he didn't finish it and left early. People said that Guan Zhong was useless and unable to accomplish anything. Bao Shu Ya, however, said that Guan Zhong was not useless, but rather that he had not yet met anyone who really understood him. He said that Guan Zhong was really a very talented man, but his opportunity had not yet arrived.

Finally Bao Shu Ya introduced Guan Zhong to a king. When the king heard what Bao Shu Ya had to say, he employed Guan Zhong as his prime minister. While Guan Zhong was serving the king, the country underwent a great change and turned into a great country. Guan Zhong was very grateful to Bao Shu Ya. He said, "My parents gave birth to me and raised me, but the one who really knew me and helped me is Bao Shu Ya. He is a true friend!"

The Emperors Yao and Shun

In ancient times, there was a legendary emperor who was very virtuous and whose name was Yao. Yao is a very famous historical person because he had such a good heart and brought a lot of happiness to people's lives. He never spent the country's or the people's money frivolously; instead, he made a great effort to help the country and the people. During his reign as emperor, the people were very satisfied and there was peace in the country. It is said that this was one of the best periods in Chinese history.

Yao had ten sons, but his eldest son had been disobedient since childhood. He didn't like to study, he only liked to play. He was not kind to the people, he did not resemble his father. Yao was very worried about his son and tried many methods to influence him in a positive way. This is why Yao invented "Wei Qi" (Go) in order to let his son play. He hoped that this game would teach his son how to live a better life. After playing for awhile, however, the eldest son lost interest.

In ancient China, only the emperor's eldest son could succeed his father, no one else was allowed to. When Yao saw how disobedient his eldest son was, and how much he disliked studying, he knew that he could not be emperor. If his son were to become emperor, the world would surely be transformed into a terrible state. Therefore, he decided that his eldest son would not be the emperor, and that he would not let any of his other sons be emperor either. He hoped to find a truly talented and renowned person so that when he was old, Yao would be able to rest and let another man take over.

Yao did manage to find such a man, his name was Shun. Shun was born to a common peasant's family. From childhood on, he had been capable of doing many things. He knew how to cultivate the fields and how to catch fish, and he knew how to build many things. When Yao met Shun, he liked him right away and wanted Shun to follow him and become the next emperor. However, because Shun was not the son of an emperor, he thought it would not be proper for him to become emperor. Because Shun was so unselfish, Yao liked him even more and gave Shun his own two daughters in marriage.

When Yao's eldest son heard that his father was planning to let another person become emperor, he was very angry. He rose up against his father and wanted to fight him. They did end up combating each other and when the eldest son realized that he could not defeat his father and that his own actions had been wrong, he went to the seashore and committed suicide. Shun then became emperor. This story of Yao letting Shun become emperor has been passed down to us through the ages.

第七章　牛郎織女和哭倒長城

哭倒長城

　　很久很久以前，地上有一個年輕的男子[1]，名叫牛郎[2]。牛郎沒有錢，家裏也沒有別的什麼東西。他只有一頭老牛和他在一起。每天，牛郎和老牛一起吃，一起種地，一起休息，他們成了很好的朋友。可是，日子久了，牛郎總覺得生活裏少了一件什麼事情。原來，他發現自己沒有妻子[3]。沒有人和他說話，也沒有人知道他在想什麼。所以，他覺得生活沒有意思。

這時，在天上也有一個人覺得生活沒有意思。這個人是天上的女子，是天帝[4]的女兒[5]，她的名字叫織女[6]。織女非常美麗，她每天的工作就是在天上織布[7]。天上的布就是我們每天看見的雲[8]。織女有六個姐姐，她們每天在天上織出千千萬萬美麗的雲。她們把這些漂亮的雲在不同的時間分給[9]不同地方的人。雖然七姐妹的生活是美麗的，可是織女總覺得生活沒有意思，但她不知道是為什麼。

有一天，牛郎的朋友老牛突然說話了。它對牛郎說："坐在我的背上，我要帶你去見美麗的七姐妹。她們中間有一位是織女，你要和她結婚"牛郎太高興了。經過老牛的介紹，牛郎和織女見面認識了。牛郎非常喜歡織女，織女也非常喜歡牛郎。織女這時才知道，她以前覺得生活沒有意思是因為什麼了。

牛郎和織女就結婚了。他們在一起生活了十年，地上的十年就是天上的十天。他們生了一個男孩，一個女孩。在地上的日子，織女就不能再織雲了，她只能織布。她織出來的布，也是非常非常的美麗，就像他們現在的生活十分美麗一樣。

可是，織女在地上結婚的事被天帝知道了。天帝很不高興，因為織女十天沒有為天上織雲了，在這十天中，天上的風景變得很不好看。所以，天帝就叫人把織女帶回天上來。那天，牛郎在外面種地[10]，突然聽見兒子和女兒一邊跑，一邊叫著說："媽媽被帶走了！媽媽被帶走了！"牛郎一看，看見織女被帶到了半空中[11]。她一邊哭，一邊對著牛郎說："我不要回去！我不要回去！"

牛郎馬上帶著兒子和女兒一起去追[12]織女，他們一直追到了天上。天帝看見牛郎追得越來越近了，就開了一條河在牛郎和織女的中間[13]，叫他們永遠不能在一起，也永遠不能再見面。這時，他們的兒女就叫著說："爸爸！我們來把河水舀乾[14]！"他們就一點一點地舀起河水來。

天帝看見他們這麼相愛[15]，就不再生氣了。可是因為織女是天上的人，所以她不能再回到地上。天帝為了讓他們可以有見面的機會，他答應[16]在每年的七月七日，讓他們一家人在一起。每年的這個時候，當人們在晚上看星星的時候，你可以看到牛郎和織女，還有他們的兒女在一起呢！

哭倒[17]長城

中國歷史上有一個很有名的故事，是說到夫妻相愛的。這個故事的名字，叫孟姜女哭倒長城。說的是秦始皇那個時候的事情。那時候，有一個女子名叫孟姜女。她剛結婚三天，丈夫就被皇帝手下的人抓[18]去造長城。一去就是很長的時間，也沒有聽到什麼消息[19]。

　　天氣慢慢變冷了，孟姜女不知道自己的丈夫[20]怎麼樣了。也不知道丈夫現在的衣服夠不夠。她很想去看看自己的丈夫。所以，她就帶上了衣服，和別的東西上路[21]了。一路上，孟姜女走得非常不容易。她一邊走，一邊找，不知道過了多少天，才走到了長城的地方。

　　可是，到了長城以後，孟姜女怎麼找，也找不到丈夫。她問了很多的人，最後才知道，她的丈夫已經死了，並且是死在長城的底下[22]。這時，孟姜女大哭起來。她哭得很難過，哭了很長很長的時間。結果，長城突然“轟”的一聲，倒下了四十多里。這時，孟姜女從倒下的長城底下，找到了自己死去的丈夫。後來，孟姜女因為太難過了，覺得活著沒有意思，就跳到[23]一條河裏自殺了。

閱讀理解

一、　牛郎為什麼覺得生活沒意思？

二、　織女是誰？

三、　牛郎和織女是怎樣結婚的？

四、　為什麼織女不要回天上去？

五、　孟姜女是誰？她和織女有什麼相同？有什麼不同？

六、　讀了孟姜女的故事，你對長城有什麼新的看法？

生字

1 男子	nánzi	ㄋㄢˊ ㄗ·	*man*
2 牛郎	niúláng	ㄋㄧㄡˊ ㄌㄤˊ	*cow herd*
3 妻子	qīzi	ㄑㄧ ㄗ·	*wife*
4 天帝	tiāndì	ㄊㄧㄢ ㄉㄧˋ	*god*
5 女兒	nǚér	ㄋㄩˇ ㄦˊ	*daughter*
6 織女	zhīnǚ	ㄓ ㄋㄩˇ	*weaver girl*
7 織布	zhībù	ㄓ ㄅㄨˋ	*to weave cloth*
8 雲	yún	ㄩㄣˊ	*cloud*
9 分給	fēngěi	ㄈㄣ ㄍㄟˇ	*to distribute*
10 種地	zhòngdì	ㄓㄨㄥˋ ㄉㄧˋ	*to farm; to cultivate the land*
11 半空中	bànkōngzhōng	ㄅㄢˋ ㄎㄨㄥ ㄓㄨㄥ	*in mid-air*
12 追	zhuī	ㄓㄨㄟ	*to chase*
13 中間	zhōngjiān	ㄓㄨㄥ ㄐㄧㄢ	*between; among*
14 舀干	yǎogān	ㄧㄠˇ ㄍㄢ	*to ladle out; to scoop*
15 相愛	xiāngài	ㄒㄧㄤ ㄞˋ	*to love each other*
16 答應	dāyìng	ㄉㄚ ㄧㄥˋ	*to allow*
17 倒	dǎo	ㄉㄠˇ	*to topple; to fall*
18 抓	zhuā	ㄓㄨㄚ	*to seize*
19 消息	xiāoxī	ㄒㄧㄠ ㄒㄧˊ	*news*
20 丈夫	zhàngfū	ㄓㄤˋ ㄈㄨ	*husband*
21 上路	shànglù	ㄕㄤˋ ㄌㄨˋ	*to set out*
22 底下	dǐxià	ㄉㄧˇ ㄒㄧㄚˋ	*under; below*
23 跳到	tiàodào	ㄊㄧㄠˋ ㄉㄠˋ	*to run to*

第七章　牛郎织女和哭倒长城

很久很久以前，地上有一个年轻的男子[1]，名叫牛郎[2]。牛郎没有钱，家里也没有别的什麽东西。他只有一头老牛和他在一起。每天，牛郎和老牛一起吃，一起种地，一起休息，他们成了很好的朋友。可是，日子久了，牛郎总觉得生活里少了一件什麽事情。原来，他发现自己没有妻子[3]。没有人和他说话，也没有人知道他在想什麽。所以，他觉得生活没有意思。

这时，在天上也有一个人觉得生活没有意思。这个人是天上的女子，是天帝[4]的女儿[5]，她的名字叫织女[6]。织女非常美丽，她每天的工作就是在天上织布[7]。天上的布就是我们每天看见的云[8]。织女有六个姐姐，她们每天在天上织出千千万万美丽的云。她们把这些漂亮的云在不同的时间分给[9]不同地方的人。虽然七姐妹的生活是美丽的，可是织女总觉得生活没有意思，但她不知道是为什麽。

有一天，牛郎的朋友老牛突然说话了。它对牛郎说："坐在我的背上，我要带你去见美丽的七姐妹。她们中间有一位是织女，你要和她结婚"牛郎太高兴了。经过老牛的介绍，牛郎和织女见面认识了。牛郎非常喜欢织女，织女也非常喜欢牛郎。织女这时才知道，她以前觉得生活没有意思是因为什麽了。

牛郎和织女就结婚了。他们在一起生活了十年，地上的十年就是天上的十天。他们生了一个男孩，一个女孩。在地上的日子，织女就不能再织云了，她只能织布。她织出来的布，也是非常非常的美丽，就像他们现在的生活十分美丽一样。

可是，织女在地上结婚的事被天帝知道了。天帝很不高兴，因为织女十天没有为天上织云了，在这十天中，天上的风景变得很不好看。所以，天帝就叫人把织女带回天上来。那天，牛郎在外面种地[10]，突然听见儿子和女儿一边跑，一边叫著说："妈妈被带走了！妈妈被带走了！"牛郎一看，看见织女被带到了半空中[11]。她一边哭，一边对著牛郎说："我不要回去！我不要回去！"

牛郎马上带著儿子和女儿一起去追[12]织女，他们一直追到了天上。天帝看见牛郎追得越来越近了，就开了一条河在牛郎和织女的中间[13]，叫他们永远不能在一起，也永远不能再见面。这时，他们的儿女就叫著说："爸爸！我们来把河水舀乾[14]！"他们就一点一点地舀起河水来。

天帝看见他们这麽相爱[15]，就不再生气了。可是因为织女是天上的人，所以她不能再回到地上。天帝为了让他们可以有见面的机会，他答应[16]在每年的七月七日，让他们一家人在一起。

每年的这个时候，当人们在晚上看星星的时候，你可以看到牛郎和织女，还有他们的儿女在一起呢！

哭倒[17]长城

中国历史上有一个很有名的故事，是说到夫妻相爱的。这个故事的名字，叫孟姜女哭倒长城。说的是秦始皇那个时候的事情。那时候，有一个女子名叫孟姜女。她刚结婚三天，丈夫就被皇帝手下的人抓[18]去造长城。一去就是很长的时间，也没有听到什麼消息[19]。

天气慢慢变冷了，孟姜女不知道自己的丈夫[20]怎麼样了。也不知道丈夫现在的衣服够不够。她很想去看看自己的丈夫。所以，她就带上了衣服，和别的东西上路[21]了。一路上，孟姜女走得非常不容易。她一边走，一边找，不知道过了多少天，才走到了长城的地方。

可是，到了长城以後，孟姜女怎麼找，也找不到丈夫。她问了很多的人，最後才知道，她的丈夫已经死了，并且是死在长城的底下[22]。这时，孟姜女大哭起来。她哭得很难过，哭了很长很长的时间。结果，长城突然"轰"的一声，倒下了四十多里。这时，孟姜女从倒下的长城底下，找到了自己死去的丈夫。後来，孟姜女因为太难过了，觉得活著没有意思，就跳到[23]一条河里自杀了。

阅读理解

一、　牛郎为什麽觉得生活没意思？

二、　织女是谁？

三、　牛郎和织女是怎样结婚的？

四、　为什麽织女不要回天上去？

五、　孟姜女是谁？她和织女有什麽相同？有什麽不同？

六、　读了孟姜女的故事，你对长城有什麽新的看法？

生字

1	男子	nánzi	man
2	牛郎	niúláng	cow herd
3	妻子	qīzi	wife
4	天帝	tiāndì	god
5	女儿	nǚér	daughter
6	织女	zhīnǚ	weaver girl
7	织布	zhībù	to weave cloth
8	云	yún	cloud
9	分给	fēngěi	to distribute
10	种地	zhòngdì	to farm; to cultivate the land
11	半空中	bànkōngzhōng	in mid-air
12	追	zhuī	to chase
13	中间	zhōngjiān	between; among
14	舀干	yǎogān	to ladle out; to scoop
15	相爱	xiāngài	to love each other
16	答应	dāyìng	to allow
17	倒	dǎo	to topple; to fall
18	抓	zhuā	to seize
19	消息	xiāoxī	news
20	丈夫	zhàngfū	husband
21	上路	shànglù	to set out
22	底下	dǐxià	under; below
23	跳到	tiàodào	to run to

Chapter 7　Niu Lang and Zhi Nu (The Cowherd and the Weaver Girl) and Tears Topple the Great Wall

A long, long time ago there was a young man whose name was Niu Lang. Niu Lang was very poor, his house was quite empty. All he had was an old cow who lived with him. Everyday Niu Lang and the old cow ate together, cultivated the land together, and rested together. They were very good friends. But as time passed, Niu Lang kept thinking that something was missing in his life. He realized that he didn't have a wife, he had no one to talk to, and nobody who knew what he was thinking about. His life seemed dull.

At the same time, up in heaven, there was someone else who thought that life was not very interesting. This person was a child from heaven, she was god's daughter. She was called Zhi Nu. Zhi Nu was very beautiful, her daily job in heaven was to weave cloth. The clouds we see everyday are really cloth woven in heaven. Zhi Nu had six sisters. They all spent everyday up in heaven weaving hundreds of thousands of beautiful clouds. They sent these lovely clouds to people in different places at different times. Although the seven sisters had a beautiful life, the weaver girl still felt that her life was dull and she didn't know why.

One day Niu Lang's friend, the old cow, said to him, "Sit on my back, I'm going to take you to see seven beautiful sisters. Among them is Zhi Nu, whom you are going to marry." Niu Lang was very excited. Old cow introduced Niu Lang and Zhi Nu and they got to know each other. Niu Lang really liked Zhi Nu and Zhi Nu really liked Niu Lang. At this point, Zhi Nu finally understood why life had seemed so dull.

Niu Lang and Zhi Nu got married. They lived together for ten years; ten years on earth are ten days in heaven. They gave birth to one son and one daughter. While she was on earth, Zhi Nu could not weave clouds, she could only weave cloth. The cloth she wove was lovely, it seemed as beautiful as the life they were living.

Unfortunately, god found out that Zhi Nu had gotten married on earth. He was not happy about it because for ten days Zhi Nu hadn't been weaving clouds for heaven, and during those ten days the landscape in heaven had become unsightly. God ordered his people to bring Zhi Nu back to heaven. On that day, Niu Lang was outside farming when he suddenly heard is son and daughter running and shouting, "Mama has been taken away! Mama has been taken away!" Just then Niu Lang saw Zhi Nu being carried through the sky. She was crying and saying to Niu Lang, "I don't want to go back! I don't want to go back!" Niu Lang took his son and daughter and went after Zhi Nu. They followed her all the way to heaven. God saw that Niu Lang was getting closer and closer so he opened up a river between Zhi Nu and Niu Lang and told them that they would never be able to be together or see each other again. Just then their children shouted, "Papa! Let's ladle the water from the river!" So they ladled the water out little by little.

When god saw how much they loved each other, he couldn't be angry any longer. However, because Zhi Nu was from heaven, she was not allowed to return to earth. In order to give them an opportunity to see each other again, god allowed the family to be together once a year on the seventh day of the seventh month. Every year on this day, when people look up at the stars at night, they can see Niu Lang and Zhi Nu and their two children reunited!

Tears Topple the Great Wall

There is a famous story in Chinese history which tells of the love between a husband and his wife. The story is called "Meng Jiang Nu's Tears Topple the Great Wall." The story takes place during Qin Shi Huang's reign. At that time, there was a girl called Meng Jiang Nu. She had been married for just three days when the emperor's men seized her husband and sent him to build the Great Wall. Once he was gone, there was no news for a very long time.

The weather gradually became cold and Meng Jiang Nu didn't know how her husband was doing. She didn't know whether her husband had enough clothes either. She wanted to see him very much, so she took some clothes and other things and set out. It was a difficult trip, and as she walked she searched for him. Nobody knows how long it took until she finally arrived at the Great Wall.

No matter how hard Meng Jiang Nu looked, however, she couldn't find her husband. She asked many people until she finally found out that he had already died. He had died under the Great Wall. Meng Jiang Nu burst into tears; she was overcome by sorrow and cried and cried for a very long time. All at once the Great Wall let out a loud rumble and a section of the wall, forty li long, toppled over. Meng Jiang Nu found her husband's body under the wall that had tumbled down. Meng Jiang Nu was so overwhelmed by her sadness that she did not want to go on living and ran into a river and drowned.

第八章　孔融讓梨和曹植寫詩[1]

曹植寫詩

　　從前有一個小孩，名叫孔融。他是中國古代的思想家和教育家－孔子的後代，是孔子的二十代孫子[2]。孔融有哥哥和弟弟一共六個。他是老六[3]，下面還有一個弟弟。他從小就很聰明，很多人喜歡他，是個很可愛的小孩子。

　　孔融四歲的時候，他的家經常有朋友送梨[4]來。這種梨是很有名的一種梨，出在中國的山東[5]，又甜[6]，又香[7]，又大，又好吃。每次朋友送梨來的時候，孔融和哥哥、弟弟們都非常高興。他們在吃以前，等得很高興，吃完了以後，玩得又很高興。當然，吃梨的時候，他們更是高興。

　　可是，每次開始吃梨的時候，哥哥和弟弟們都會有些麻煩。因為大家都想吃大的梨，所以每次哥哥和弟弟們總是要搶[8]梨吃，所以每次總會有一些不高興。但孔融每次都不搶，總是最後一個去拿梨。為了搶梨這件事，母親常常教育孩子們，應該學習讓別人。後來，母親每次就要年紀小的弟弟先拿，年紀大的哥哥後拿。

　　奇怪的是，每次孔融都是拿最小的梨吃。母親每次看見，心裏不明白。她就問孔融說："孩子，你是不是不喜歡吃梨呢？要不然，你怎麼每次都拿小的梨吃呢？"孔融回答說："因為我年紀小，應該吃小的。哥哥們年紀大，吃的比我多，所以他們應該吃大的。"家裏的人聽了，覺得非常奇怪，這麼小的年紀，怎麼會知道這些事情呢？

　　孔融因為從小就很聰明，而且在很多事情上肯[9]學習，後來，他成了漢朝[10]一位很有名的文學家。他是當時七位最有名的文學家[11]之一。孔融讓梨的故事，成了中國許許多多的父母教育孩子的很好的故事。

曹植寫詩

在中國的三國時代，整個中國分成了三個國家，所以叫做三國。在這三個國家裏，有一個國家的國王叫曹操。曹操有四個兒子，大兒子叫曹丕。曹操死了以後，曹丕就接著作了國王。

在中國，幾千年來有一個傳統，就是父母如果去世[12]了，兒女一定要回去見最後一面。如果兒女不回去，這將是人生[13]的大罪[14]。所以，不管發生了什麼事情，也不管離開家有多遠，父母去世的時候，兒女是必須回去的。

可是，當曹操王死了以後，他的兒子曹植卻沒有回去見父親最後一面。曹植和幾位朋友反而在家裏喝酒、玩，好像父親沒有死一樣。哥哥曹丕現在作了國王。他聽到弟弟在喝酒，不來見父親最後一面，就非常生氣。他就要抓弟弟曹植問罪[15]。

他們的母親聽說了這件事，她知道哥哥曹丕很不喜歡弟弟曹植，知道不好[16]。可能哥哥想用這次機會來殺弟弟。母親就說："你弟弟知道自己很有才能，但不能接你父親作王，所以心裏不高興。他不是故意不來見你父親最後一面的。你

是不是可以不要殺你的弟弟。"曹丕就對母親說："請母親
放心，我有辦法的。"

曹植被帶到曹丕王的面前，他知道自己是要死的。所以，
他就向曹丕請罪[17]。曹丕對弟弟說："你雖然是我的弟弟，
可是你已經得罪了[18]國家的王法[19]。現在我給你一個機會。別
人都說你很有天才，很會寫詩。如果你走七步可以作出一首
詩來，你就可以不死。"曹植回答說："我願意試試，請哥
哥給我一個題目。"曹丕王說："題目就是哥哥和弟弟。可
是，詩的裏面不可以出現哥哥和弟弟這兩個字。"

曹植聽了就開始走，七步還沒有走完，詩就寫出來了。
這首詩是這樣的：

喝的湯[20]是用豆子煮[21]的，濾出[22]豆子後就成了湯汁[23]，
煮豆子的火是用豆萁[24]燒的，豆子在鍋子裏非常難過[25]，豆
子和豆萁本是一家，為什麼自己燒自己要這麼急呢？

曹丕王聽了以後，感動[26]得哭了，他就免了[27]弟弟的罪和
死。

註：原詩為：煮(cook)豆(bean)持作(to make)羹(soup)，漉(filter)
菽(bean)以為(as)汁(juice)，萁(beanstalk)在釜(pot)下然(burn)，
豆(bean)在釜(pot)中泣(cry)，本自(from)同根(root)生(born)，相
煎(boil)何(why)太(so)急(hastily)。

閱讀理解：

一、 孔融是誰？

二、 孔融爲什麼每次總是拿小的梨子？

三、 孔融爲什麼每次不去搶梨子？

四、 後來孔融成了一個什麼樣的人？

五、 曹操是誰？

六、 曹植爲什麼不去見父親的最後一面？

七、 哥哥曹丕爲什麼要抓弟弟曹植問罪？

八、 請用你自己的話，說出七步詩的意思。

九、 爲什麼曹丕免了弟弟的罪？

生字

[1] 詩	shī	ㄕ	*poem*
[2] 孫子	sūnzi	ㄙㄨㄣ ㄗ˙	*grand-son*
[3] 老六	lǎoliù	ㄌㄠˇ ㄌㄧㄡˋ	*the sixth child*
[4] 梨	lí	ㄌㄧˊ	*pear*
[5] 山東	shāndōng	ㄕㄢ ㄉㄨㄥ	*province in China*
[6] 甜	tián	ㄊㄧㄢˊ	*sweet*
[7] 香	xiāng	ㄒㄧㄤ	*fragrant*
[8] 搶	qiǎng	ㄑㄧㄤˇ	*to grab*
[9] 肯	kěn	ㄎㄣˇ	*to agree; to consent*

[10] 漢朝	hàncháo	ㄏㄢˋ ㄔㄠˊ	the Han Dynasty
[11] 文學家	wénxuéjiā	ㄨㄣˊ ㄒㄩㄝˊ ㄐㄧㄚ	writer
[12] 去世	qùshì	ㄑㄩˋ ㄕˋ	to die
[13] 人生	rénshēng	ㄖㄣˊ ㄕㄥ	life
[14] 大罪	dàzuì	ㄉㄚˋ ㄗㄨㄟˋ	a great crime
[15] 問罪	wènzuì	ㄨㄣˋ ㄗㄨㄟˋ	to put on trial
[16] 知道不好	zhīdàobùhǎo	ㄓ ㄉㄠˋ ㄅㄨˋ ㄏㄠˇ	to know that something is wrong
[17] 請罪	qǐngzuì	ㄑㄧㄥˇ ㄗㄨㄟˋ	to admit one's error
[18] 得罪了	dézuìle	ㄉㄜˊ ㄗㄨㄟˋ ㄌㄜ·	to offend
[19] 王法	wángfǎ	ㄨㄤˊ ㄈㄚˇ	the law of the land
[20] 湯	tāng	ㄊㄤ	soup
[21] 煮	zhǔ	ㄓㄨˇ	to cook
[22] 濾出	lǜchū	ㄌㄩˋ ㄔㄨ	to strain
[23] 湯汁	tāngzhī	ㄊㄤ ㄓ	liquid soup
[24] 豆萁	dòuqí	ㄉㄡˋ ㄑㄧˊ	beanstalks
[25] 難過	nánguò	ㄋㄢˊ ㄍㄨㄛˋ	miserable
[26] 感動	gǎndòng	ㄍㄢˇ ㄉㄨㄥˋ	to be moved
[27] 免了	miǎnle	ㄇㄧㄢˇ ㄌㄜ·	to forgive

第八章　孔融让梨和曹植写诗[1]

从前有一个小孩，名叫孔融。他是中国古代的思想家和教育家－孔子的後代，是孔子的二十代孙子[2]。孔融有哥哥和弟弟一共六个。他是老六[3]，下面还有一个弟弟。他从小就很聪明，很多人喜欢他，是个很可爱的小孩子。

孔融四岁的时候，他的家经常有朋友送梨[4]来。这种梨是很有名的一种梨，出在中国的山东[5]，又甜[6]，又香[7]，又大，又好吃。每次朋友送梨来的时候，孔融和哥哥、弟弟们都非常高兴。他们在吃以前，等得很高兴，吃完了以後，玩得又很高兴。当然，吃梨的时候，他们更是高兴。

可是，每次开始吃梨的时候，哥哥和弟弟们都会有些麻烦。因为大家都想吃大的梨，所以每次哥哥和弟弟们总是要抢[8]梨吃，所以每次总会有一些不高兴。但孔融每次都不抢，总是最後一个去拿梨。为了抢梨这件事，母亲常常教育孩子们，应该学习让别人。後来，母亲每次就要年纪小的弟弟先拿，年纪大的哥哥後拿。

奇怪的是，每次孔融都是拿最小的梨吃。母亲每次看见，心里不明白。她就问孔融说："孩子，你是不是不喜欢吃梨呢？要不然，你怎麼每次都拿小的梨吃呢？"孔融回答说："因为我年纪小，应该吃小的。哥哥们年纪大，吃的比我多，所以他们应该吃大的。"家里的人听了，觉得非常奇怪，这麼小的年纪，怎麼会知道这些事情呢？

孔融因为从小就很聪明，而且在很多事情上肯[9]学习，後来，他成了汉朝[10]一位很有名的文学家。他是当时七位最有名的文学家[11]之一。孔融让梨的故事，成了中国许许多多的父母教育孩子的很好的故事。

曹植写诗

在中国的三国时代，整个中国分成了三个国家，所以叫做三国。在这三个国家里，有一个国家的国王叫曹操。曹操有四个儿子，大儿子叫曹丕。曹操死了以後，曹丕就接著作了国王。

在中国，几千年来有一个传统，就是父母如果去世[12]了，儿女一定要回去见最後一面。如果儿女不回去，这将是人生[13]的大罪[14]。所以，不管发生了什麼事情，也不管离开家有多远，父母去世的时候，儿女是必须回去的。

可是，当曹操王死了以後，他的儿子曹植却没有回去见父亲最後一面。曹植和几位朋友反而在家里喝酒、玩，好像父亲他们的母亲听说了这件事，她知道哥哥曹丕很不喜欢弟弟曹植，知道不好[16]。可能哥哥想用这次机会来杀弟弟。母亲就说："你弟弟知道自己很有才能，但不能接你父亲作王，所以心里不高兴。他不是故意不来见你父亲最後一面的。你是不是可以不要杀你的弟弟。"曹丕就对母亲说："请母亲放心，我有办法的。"

曹植被带到曹丕王的面前，他知道自己是要死的。所以，他就向曹丕请罪[17]。曹丕对弟弟说："你虽然是我的弟弟，可是你已经得罪了[18]国家的王法[19]。现在我给你一个机会。别人都说你很有天才，很会写诗。如果你走七步可以作出一首诗来，你就可以不死。"曹植回答说："我愿意试试，请哥哥给我一个题目。"曹丕王说："题目就是哥哥和弟弟。可是，诗的里面不可以出现哥哥和弟弟这两个字。"

曹植听了就开始走，七步还没有走完，诗就写出来了。这首诗是这样的：

喝的汤[20]是用豆子煮[21]的，滤出[22]豆子後就成了汤汁[23]，煮豆子的火是用豆萁[24]烧的，豆子在锅子里非常难过[25]，豆子和豆萁本是一家，为什麽自己烧自己要这麽急呢？

曹丕王听了以後，感动[26]得哭了，他就免了[27]弟弟的罪和死。

注：原诗为：煮(cook)豆(bean)持作(to make)羹(soup)，漉(filter)菽(bean)以为(as)汁(juice)，其(beanstalk)在釜(pot)下然(burn)，豆(bean)在釜(pot)中泣(cry)，本自(from)同根(root)生(born)，相煎(boil)何(why)太(so)急(hastily)。

阅读理解：

一、 孔融是谁？

二、 孔融为什麽每次总是拿小的梨子？

三、 孔融为什麽每次不去抢梨子？

四、 後来孔融成了一个什麽样的人？

五、 曹操是谁？

六、 曹植为什麽不去见父亲的最後一面？

七、 哥哥曹丕为什麽要抓弟弟曹植问罪？

八、 请用你自己的话，说出七步诗的意思。

九、 为什麽曹丕免了弟弟的罪？

生字

1	诗	shī	poem
2	孙子	sūnzi	grand-son
3	老六	lǎoliù	the sixth child
4	梨	lí	pear
5	山东	shāndōng	province in China
6	甜	tián	sweet
7	香	xiāng	fragrant
8	抢	qiǎng	to grab
9	肯	kěn	to agree; to consent
10	汉朝	hàncháo	the Han Dynasty
11	文学家	wénxuéjiā	writer
12	去世	qùshì	to die
13	人生	rénshēng	life
14	大罪	dàzuì	a great crime
15	问罪	wènzuì	to put on trial
16	知道不好	zhīdàobùhǎo	to know that something is wrong
17	请罪	qǐngzuì	to admit one's error
18	得罪了	dézuìle	to offend
19	王法	wángfǎ	the law of the land
20	汤	tāng	soup
21	煮	zhǔ	to cook
22	滤出	lùchū	to strain
23	汤汁	tāngzhī	liquid soup
24	豆其	dòuqí	beanstalks
25	难过	nánguò	miserable
26	感动	gǎndòng	to be moved
27	免了	miǎnle	to forgive

Chapter 8   Kong Rong Gives Up the Big Pear and the Story of Cao Zhi

There once was a boy named Kong Rong. He was a twenty-second generation descendant of Confucius, the ancient Chinese philosopher and educator. Kong Rong had six brothers. Kong Rong was the sixth, with one younger brother. From childhood on, Kong Rong had been very intelligent and very well-liked by everyone; he was a sweet boy.

When he was four-years-old, there were often friends who brought pears as a present. The pears were famous pears grown in China's Shandong Province; they were sweet, fragrant, large, and delicious. Whenever friends came and brought pears, Kong Rong and his brothers were very happy. Before eating them, they waited happily, and after eating them they played happily too. Of course, they were happiest while eating the pears.

However, every time they started eating the pears, a problem arose among the brothers. Everybody wanted to eat the biggest pear, so the brothers always scrambled to get it and someone was always left feeling unhappy. Kong Rong, on the other hand, did not grab, he always helped himself last. Their mother kept trying to teach them not to grab the pears so they could learn to let others go first. She ended up letting the youngest brothers choose first and the older brothers choose afterwards.

Strangely, Kong Rong always chose the smallest pear. When his mother saw this, she didn't understand and asked Kong Rong, "Do you not like pears, child? Why else would you always choose the smallest?" Kong Rong answered, "I am young, I should eat less. My brothers are older, they eat more than I do and should eat the bigger pears." His family was very surprised when they heard this; how could such a young person know about such things?

Because Kong Rong was so intelligent and agreed to study all sorts of things, he later became a famous writer of the Han Dynasty. He was one of seven famous writers of that time. The story of Kong giving up the big pear has been used by many parents in China to teach their children.

Cao Zhi Writes a Poem

During the period of the Three Kingdoms, China was divided into three countries and was therefore called the Three Kingdoms. In one of the three countries was a king named Cao Cao. Cao Cao had four sons, his eldest was called Cao Pi. When Cao Cao died, Cao Pi succeeded him and became king.

There is a legend which is several thousand years old that says that when parents die, the children must come back to see them one more time. Failing to return home was considered a great crime. So, no matter what, and no matter how far from home they are, when parents die, the children must return home.

However, when King Cao Cao died, his son Cao Zhi did not return home to see his father one last time. Instead, Cao Zhi stayed at his home, drinking and playing around with his friends, acting as if his father had not died at all. His elder brother Cao Pi was now the king. He became very angry when he heard that his brother had been drinking instead of paying his father one last visit. He wanted to put his brother Cao Zhi on trial for this.

When their mother heard about the trial, she knew it was wrong, she knew that Cao Pi didn't like his younger brother Cao Zhi. She thought that Cao Pi might use this excuse to kill his younger brother. She said, "Your younger brother knows that he is very talented but he also knows that he cannot be king, that is why he is so unhappy. It was not on purpose that he didn't come to see his father one last time. Please do not kill your younger brother." Cao Pi said to his mother, "Please do not worry, Mother. I have a solution."   When Cao Zhi was brought in front of King Cao Pi, he knew that he had been condemned to death. He admitted his error and asked for forgiveness. Cao Pi said to his brother, "Although you are my younger brother, you have offended the law of the land. I am going to give you one chance. Others tell me that you are very talented and a good poet. If you can make a poem while taking seven steps, you will not have to die." Cao Zhi answered, "I would like to try, but please, elder brother, give me a topic." Cao Pi said, "The subject is elder and younger brothers. However, the words, 'elder brother' and 'younger brother' may not be mentioned in the poem."

As soon as Cao Zhi heard this, he started walking. He hadn't even taken his seventh step when he had already written the following poem:

Beans are used to cook soup,
The beans are strained out to make soup.
Beanstalks are used to light the fire which cooks the beans.
The beans in the soup feel miserable,
Beans and beanstalks are of one family.
Why does one burn the other so hastily?

When King Cao Pi heard this poem, he was so moved that he cried. He pardoned his brother and canceled his death sentence.

第九章　借光讀書的故事

中國人有一個傳統[1]，就是特別注意小孩子的教育。

古時候，許多的父母雖然沒有錢，他們還是想出所有的辦法，讓小孩子去讀書。當然，父母這樣作是非常好的一件事情，因為可以使小孩子多接受一點教育。

可是，如果一個小孩子自己喜歡讀書，那真是一件最好不過的事[2]了。下面的幾個故事，就是古時候的小孩子自己用功讀書的故事。這些故事都是發生在很久很久以前。那時候，中國人的生活是很窮[3]的。可是，這些孩子讀書的精神，卻是在現在的人身上[4]很少能見到的。

借光讀書

漢朝的時候，有一個孩子。他很喜歡讀書。可是他的家裏沒有錢，他就只好白天去做工。白天做了一整天的工，人非常累了。只有晚上才能休息。可是一到晚上，他也不放過[5]機會看書。但因為家裏沒有錢買燈[6]和油，所以他到了晚上，還是沒有燈光可以看書。

有一天，他回家的時候，天已經黑了。進了家門，他突然發現有光從牆[7]上照過來。他走近一看，發現原來牆上有一個洞[8]。屋子裏的光就是從這個洞裏照出來的。那是從鄰居家照過來的燈光。這孩子一見，太高興了。他就坐在牆洞邊，借著光，讀起書來。從這以後，他每天白天工作，晚上回來以後，就坐在牆洞邊借光讀書。

螢蟲[9]作燈

很久很久以前，有一個小孩子姓車，只有十歲。可是他知道的事情特別多。好像他在什麼地方，讀了不少的書。他的朋友和鄰居[10]都很奇怪，因為他的家很窮，他必須每天做很多的事。怎麼能去讀書呢？他們很想看看，他在家裏到底作什麼。

到他的家裏一看，才知道小孩子每天晚上都在家裏讀書。可是，他家裏很窮，怎麼有錢買燈和油來讀書呢？大家這時才發現，孩子的家裏沒有燈。可是，他沒有燈怎麼能讀書呢？

後來他們才發現，在夏天的時候，這個小孩子每天晚上就去屋子的外面捉螢火蟲[11]。他捉了很多很多的螢火蟲，就把它們放在一個袋子[12]裏。這樣，螢火蟲在袋子裏就像一隻小油燈一樣的光明。小孩子每天晚上就在螢火蟲的光底下讀起書來。

雪[13]冷光明

古時候，有一個小男孩姓孫，家裏很窮。可是他很喜歡讀書。冬天下雪的時候，每家都是把門窗關[14]得緊緊的，怕有風進來。可是，這個小男孩睡在屋子裏，總是不關窗子[15]。家裏的人和鄰居都很奇怪，問他下雪[16]的天這麼冷，為什麼不關窗子睡覺[17]。小男孩說：“因為我打開窗子，就可以借著外面雪地發出的光[18]來看書。”大家聽了都非常感動，因為他是一個愛讀書的孩子。

人高得月

　　還有一個故事，說的是有位姓江的小孩子用功讀書的事情。這個小孩子讀書的時候也是在晚上。他的家裏也是沒有錢買燈和油。所以，他讀書的時候是借著月光來看的。

　　可是，月光一點一點在走動[19]。過了不久，月光就被房子、樹、或者別的東西擋住[20]了。這時候，小孩子就要走到月光沒有被擋住的地方去，在那裏繼續讀書。但是，這樣作很不方便，因為有的時候月亮被擋住的時候，他需要走到離開房子很遠的地方去。所以，小孩子就開始想辦法，希望可以很容易地借月光讀書。

　　最後，他想出了一個好辦法。到了晚上的時候，他就搬了一個梯子[21]來，靠著[22]房子的牆。他就坐在梯子上看書。等月光被東西擋住了的時候，他就往上爬[23]一級[24]，再繼續看書。再擋住了，就再往上爬一級，再繼續看。這樣，一級一級，月光就不再會被擋住了。

閱讀理解：

一、　中國人為什麼特別注意小孩子的教育？

二、　本文中的四個小孩子讀書有什麼相同？有什麼不同？

三、　猜猜看，為什麼這些小孩子喜歡讀書？

四、　現代的小孩子喜看書嗎？為什麼？

生字

1	傳統	chuántǒng	ㄔㄨㄢˊ ㄊㄨㄥˇ	*tradition*
2	最好不過的事	zuìhǎobúguò deshì	ㄗㄨㄟˋ ㄏㄠˇ ㄅㄨˊ ㄍㄨㄛˋ ㄉㄜ˙ ㄕˋ	*nothing could be better*
3	窮	qióng	ㄑㄩㄥˊ	*poor*
4	身上	shēnshang	ㄕㄣ ㄕㄤˋ	*oneself*
5	不放過	bùfàngguò	ㄅㄨˋ ㄈㄤˋ ㄍㄨㄛˋ	*not to forgo*
6	燈	dēng	ㄉㄥ	*light*
7	牆	qiáng	ㄑㄧㄤˊ	*wall*
8	洞	dòng	ㄉㄨㄥˋ	*hole*
9	螢蟲	yíngchóng	ㄧㄥˊ ㄔㄨㄥˊ	*firefly*
10	鄰居	línjū	ㄌㄧㄣˊ ㄐㄩ	*neighbor*
11	螢火蟲	yínghuǒchóng	ㄧㄥˊ ㄏㄨㄛˇ ㄔㄨㄥˊ	*firefly*
12	袋子	dàizi	ㄉㄞˋ ㄗ˙	*bag*
13	雪	xuě	ㄒㄩㄝˇ	*snow*
14	關	guān	ㄍㄨㄢ	*to close*
15	窗子	chuāngzi	ㄔㄨㄤ ㄗ˙	*the window*
16	下雪	xiàxuě	ㄒㄧㄚˋ ㄒㄩㄝˇ	*to snow*
17	睡覺	shuìjiào	ㄕㄨㄟˋ ㄐㄧㄠˋ	*to sleep*

[18] 發出的光	fāchūdeguāng	ㄈㄚ ㄔㄨ ㄅㄜ· ㄍㄨㄤ	*reflected light*
[19] 走動	zǒudòng	ㄗㄡˇ ㄉㄨㄥˋ	*to move*
[20] 擋住	dǎngzhù	ㄉㄤˇ ㄓㄨˋ	*to block*
[21] 梯子	tīzi	ㄊㄧ ㄗ·	*ladder*
[22] 靠著	kàozhe	ㄎㄠˋ ㄓㄜ·	*to lean against*
[23] 爬	pá	ㄆㄚˊ	*to climb*
[24] 級	jí	ㄐㄧˊ	*a rung*

第九章　借光读书的故事

中国人有一个传统[1]，就是特别注意小孩子的教育。

古时候，许多的父母虽然没有钱，他们还是想出所有的办法，让小孩子去读书。当然，父母这样作是非常好的一件事情，因为可以使小孩子多接受一点教育。

可是，如果一个小孩子自己喜欢读书，那真是一件最好不过的事[2]了。下面的几个故事，就是古时候的小孩子自己用功读书的故事。这些故事都是发生在很久很久以前。那时候，中国人的生活是很穷[3]的。可是，这些孩子读书的精神，却是在现在的人身上[4]很少能见到的。

借光读书

汉朝的时候，有一个孩子。他很喜欢读书。可是他的家里没有钱，他就只好白天去做工。白天做了一整天的工，人非常累了。只有晚上才能休息。可是一到晚上，他也不放过[5]机会看书。但因为家里没有钱买灯[6]和油，所以他到了晚上，还是没有灯光可以看书。

有一天，他回家的时候，天已经黑了。进了家门，他突然发现有光从墙[7]上照过来。他走近一看，发现原来墙上有一个洞[8]。屋子里的光就是从这个洞里照出来的。那是从邻居家照过来的灯光。这孩子一见，太高兴了。他就坐在墙洞边，借著光，读起书来。从这以後，他每天白天工作，晚上回来以後，就坐在墙洞边借光读书。

萤虫[9]作灯

很久很久以前，有一个小孩子姓车，只有十岁。可是他知道的事情特别多。好像他在什麽地方，读了不少的书。他的朋友和邻居[10]都很奇怪，因为他的家很穷，他必须每天做很多的事。怎麽能去读书呢？他们很想看看，他在家里到底作什麽。

到他的家里一看，才知道小孩子每天晚上都在家里读书。可是，他家里很穷，怎麽有钱买灯和油来读书呢？大家这时才发现，孩子的家里没有灯。可是，他没有灯怎麽能读书呢？

後来他们才发现，在夏天的时候，这个小孩子每天晚上就去屋子的外面捉萤火虫[11]。他捉了很多很多的萤火虫，就把它们放在一个袋子[12]里。这样，萤火虫在袋子里就像一只小油灯一样的光明。小孩子每天晚上就在萤火虫的光底下读起书来。

雪[13]冷光明

古时候，有一个小男孩姓孙，家里很穷。可是他很喜欢读书。冬天下雪的时候，每家都是把门窗关[14]得紧紧的，怕有风进来。可是，这个小男孩睡在屋子里，总是不关窗子[15]。家里的人和邻居都很奇怪，问他下雪[16]的天这麽冷，为什麽不关窗子睡觉[17]。小男孩说："因为我打开窗子，就可以借著外面雪地发出的光[18]来看书。"大家听了都非常感动，因为他是一个爱读书的孩子。

人高得月

还有一个故事，说的是有位姓江的小孩子用功读书的事情。这个小孩子读书的时候也是在晚上。他的家里也是没有钱买灯和油。所以，他读书的时候是借著月光来看的。

可是，月光一点一点在走动[19]。过了不久，月光就被房子、树、或者别的东西挡住[20]了。这时候，小孩子就要走到月光没有被挡住的地方去，在那里继续读书。但是，这样作很不方便，因为有的时候月亮被挡住的时候，他需要走到离开房子很远的地方去。所以，小孩子就开始想办法，希望可以很容易地借月光读书。

最後，他想出了一个好办法。到了晚上的时候，他就搬了一个梯子[21]来，靠著[22]房子的墙。他就坐在梯子上看书。等月再挡住了，就再往上爬一级，再继续看。这样，一级一级，月光就不再会被挡住了。

阅读理解：

一、 中国人为什麽特别注意小孩子的教育？

二、 本文中的四个小孩子读书有什麽相同？有什麽不同？

三、 猜猜看，为什麽这些小孩子喜欢读书？

四、 现代的小孩子喜看书吗？为什麽？

生字

1	传统	chuántǒng	tradition
2	最好不过的事	zuìhǎobúguòdeshì	nothing could be better
3	穷	qióng	poor
4	身上	shēnshang	oneself
5	不放过	bùfàngguò	not to forgo
6	灯	dēng	light
7	墙	qiáng	wall
8	洞	dòng	hole
9	萤虫	yíngchóng	firefly
10	邻居	línjū	neighbor
11	萤火虫	yínghuǒchóng	firefly
12	袋子	dàizi	bag
13	雪	xuě	snow
14	关	guān	to close
15	窗子	chuāngzi	the window
16	下雪	xiàxuě	to snow
17	睡觉	shuìjiào	to sleep
18	发出的光	fāchūdeguāng	reflected light
19	走动	zǒudòng	to move
20	挡住	dǎngzhù	to block
21	梯子	tīzi	ladder
22	靠著	kàozhe	to lean against
23	爬	pá	to climb
24	级	jí	a rung

Chapter 9   Studying by Borrowed Light

The Chinese traditionally pay great attention to their children's education. In ancient times, although many people were very poor, they still tried to come up with different ways to encourage their children to study. Indeed, it is a very good thing to make children obtain an education.

Nothing is better than a child who enjoys studying on his own accord. The following stories are about some children who studied diligently on their own. These stories all occurred a long time ago. The Chinese were very poor at the time and the studious spirit of these children living in poverty is something quite rare in our day.

Studying by Borrowed Light

During the Han Dynasty there was a child who loved to study. However, his family was very poor and so he had no choice but to go out to work everyday. After working all day long, a person is very tired and needs to rest in the evening. However, when evening came this boy didn't want to forgo his chance to read. His family, however, could not afford to buy a lamp or oil, so he had no light to read by in the evening.

One day when he came home, it was already dark. As he stepped in, he suddenly noticed light shining from the wall. He went in to look and discovered that the wall had a hole. The light in the room was coming from the hole. The light came from the neighbor's house through the hole in the wall. As soon as he saw this, the child was very excited. He sat down next to the hole and "borrowed" the light in order to read. From that day forward, he worked during the day and at night he sat by the hole in the wall, studying by borrowed light.

The Firefly Lamp

A long time ago there was a child whose family name was Ju. He was only ten-years-old, but he was very knowledgeable. From the way he talked, it seemed as if he had read many books. His friends and his neighbors were very curious. His family was very poor and he had many chores to do, how could he find time to study? They wanted to see what he actually did at home.

When they came to his home, they discovered that the child did study every evening. But the family was so poor, how could they possibly afford a lamp and oil for studying? In fact, they discovered that there was no lamp in the house. So how did he manage to study?

They discovered that the young boy went out every evening during the summer to collect fireflies. When he had caught enough fireflies, he put them into a bag. All the fireflies in the bag shone as brightly as a small oil lamp. At night the young boy sat under the light of the fireflies and studied his books.

Reflected Light on Frozen Snow

Once upon a time there was a young man named Sun who was very poor and who loved to read. In winter when it snowed, people closed their windows and doors tightly to keep the wind out. This young man, however, never closed the window in the room where he slept. His family members and neighbors thought this was strange and asked him why he didn't shut the window of his room when it was so cold outside. The young man answered, "When the window is open, I can read by the light reflected from the snow." Everyone was very moved by this boy who loved to study so much.

Climb High to Get the Moonlight

Another story tells about a studious child called Jiang. This child also studied in the evening. His family could not afford a lamp or oil either, so he studied by the light of the moon.

The light of the moon tends to move, and after just a short time, the light was blocked by a building, a tree, or something else. Then the child would go to where the light was not blocked and continue his studies. This, however, was not very convenient. Sometimes, when the light of the moon was being blocked out, he had to go very far from home. He tried to think of a better way to use the light of the moon for his reading.

Finally he had a solution. In the evening, he brought a ladder and leaned it against the wall of the house. He sat on the ladder and read. Whenever the light was blocked by something, he simply climbed up one rung and continued reading. When the light was blocked again, again he climbed up and continued his studies. That way, one rung at a time, he avoided having something block the light of the moon.

第十章　鐵杵磨針和愚公移山

鐵杵磨針

　　中國人有句古話說：“世上無難事，只怕有心人[1]。”意思是，一個人只要有決心[2]，就沒有辦[3]不到的事情。因為從古到今有很多的中國人相信這句話，所以，民間[4]就傳下來一些故事，讓人記住這個道理。當然，有的時候這些故事看起來是很笨的事情。可是，這些故事的意思是爲了叫人學習肯下決心，認真作事。下面就是兩個這樣的故事。

鐵[5]杵[6]磨[7]針[8]

中國古時候有一個大詩人，名字叫李白。傳說李白小時候不喜歡讀書，一天到晚都在外面玩。家裏的人都不知道對他該[9]怎麼辦[10]。日子[11]就這麼一天一天的過去了。

有一天，李白來到一條河邊玩。他突然發現有一位老太太也在河邊。老太太正拿著一根鐵棒[12]在石頭上磨。老太太很用心[13]的在磨，李白走近了，她也不知道。李白覺得很奇怪，就問老太太說："您在作什麼呢？"老太太看也沒看李白一眼[14]，繼續磨著鐵棒。她回答說："我要把它磨成一根針。"

李白聽了覺得更奇怪了，又問她說："這麼粗[15]的鐵棒，怎麼可能磨成針呢？"老太太說："我今天磨，明天也磨。鐵棒只會越磨越細[16]，總有一天[17]它會被我磨成針的。"

李白回家以後天天想著這件事情。他沒有辦法相信[18]世界上還有這樣一位老太太，要把鐵棒磨成針。但是他想，如果我們做事情都是這樣肯下決心，那還有什麼事情不能做成[19]呢？從這以後[20]，李白就非常用功地學習。後來，他成了一個有名的大詩人。

愚[21]公[22]移[23]山

傳說古時候在中國的北方，有兩座大山。一座叫太行山，一座叫王屋山。這兩座山非常的大，又非常的高。它們擋住[24]了南來北往[25]的去路，使人們的交通[26]和生活很不方便。

有一位老人名叫愚公，年紀已經九十歲了。他的家就是被這兩座山擋住了去路。每次愚公和家裏的人要去什麼地方，都要走很遠的彎路[27]。所以，愚公和家裏的人都覺得很不方便。

愚公就把家裏的人找來，對他們說："我們一起把這兩座山挖掉[28]，這樣我們以後就方便了。你們說怎麼樣？"大家都覺得這個想法[29]很好。愚叔叔和愚姑姑們也很同意。還有小孫子不愚搶著話說，到底[30]是爺爺年紀大，有辦法。我們愚家這麼多人，每天都住在山裏真沒有什麼意思。挖挖山不是很好玩嗎？

只有[31]愚公的妻子覺得不行。愚老太太也差不多九十歲了。她說愚公的一生都是在想一些最笨的事情做。做太太的最知道愚公是一個什麼樣的人了。她說："以前你想挖開兩個小小的土堆[32]，一直到現在都做不成。怎麼可能去挖走兩座那麼大的山呢？即使你真的能挖掉這兩座山，那些土和石頭又搬[33]到哪裏去呢？"

大家覺得愚老太太的話也很有道理，就你一言我一語[34]的談起來。三愚叔說，土和石頭可以搬到海裏去，三愚姑說那可能要搬一年的時間。小孫子不愚又搶著話說，不需要搬到海裏去。只需要把北邊的山挖到西邊，南邊的山挖到東邊就可以了。可是愚公說，以後兩座山又會擋住東西方向的去路，再要挖回來就麻煩了。最後大家還是決定把土和石頭搬到海裏去。

有一個人，姓智[35]。大家都叫他智伯。他是愚公的好朋友，只是[36]兩個人總是談不到一起。他聽說愚公不搬家，反而要搬山，覺得世界上有愚公這樣的笨人，真是少見。他一定要去跟他談一談。他就來到愚公的家，對他說：“你已經九十歲了，還能活多久呢？你這樣做，不怕天下的人笑話[37]你嗎？”

愚公回答說：“你怎麼這麼笨？我死了以後，我的兒子還會繼續挖。兒子死了，又有孫子。子子孫孫[38]是可以一直挖下去的。這兩座山卻不會變高，總有一天會被挖平的。”智伯雖然還有很多的問題，可是看到愚公這麼有決心，就不再說話了。後來，這件事感動了天上的神，神就把這兩座山搬走了。

閱讀理解：

一、　你認為這兩個故事想要教我們的是什麼？

二、　智伯後來為什麼不說話了？

三、　李白是誰？

四、　你讀過李白的詩嗎？

五、　談談你對"天下無難事，只怕有心人"的看法。

六、　在你的人生中，你見過老太太或愚公這樣的人嗎？

生字

1 有心人	yǒuxīnrén	一ㄡˇ ㄒㄧㄣ ㄖㄣˊ	to be resolved
2 決心	juéxīn	ㄐㄩㄝˊ ㄒㄧㄣ	perseverance; determination
3 辦	bàn	ㄅㄢˋ	to accomplish
4 民間	mínjiān	ㄇㄧㄣˊ ㄐㄧㄢ	folk
5 鐵	tiě	ㄊㄧㄝˇ	iron
6 杵	chǔ	ㄔㄨˇ	pestle; staff
7 磨	mó	ㄇㄛˊ	to grind
8 針	zhēn	ㄓㄣ	needle
9 該	gāi	ㄍㄞ	ought to
10 怎麼辦	zěmobàn	ㄗㄜˇ ㄇㄛ· ㄅㄢˋ	how to deal with...
11 日子	rìzi	ㄖˋ ㄗ·	the days
12 棒	bàng	ㄅㄤˋ	club; staff
13 用心	yòngxīn	ㄩㄥˋ ㄒㄧㄣ	concentrated; careful
14 看也沒看…一眼	kànyěméi kàn…yīyǎn	ㄎㄢˋ 一ㄝˇ ㄇㄟˊ ㄎㄢˋ… 一 一ㄢˇ	didn't even glance at

15	粗	cū	ㄘㄨ	thick
16	細	xì	ㄒㄧˋ	fine; thin
17	總有一天	zǒngyǒuyītiān	ㄗㄨㄥˇ ㄧㄡˇ ㄧ ㄊㄧㄢ	someday
18	相信	xiāngxìn	ㄒㄧㄤ ㄒㄧㄣˋ	to believe
19	做成	zuòchéng	ㄗㄨㄛˋ ㄔㄥˊ	to accomplish; to succeed
20	從這以後	cóngzhèyǐhòu	ㄘㄨㄥˊ ㄓㄜˋ ㄧˇ ㄏㄡˋ	from then on
21	愚	yú	ㄩˊ	foolish
22	公	gōng	ㄍㄨㄥ	Mister
23	移	yí	ㄧˊ	to move
24	擋住	dǎngzhù	ㄉㄤˇ ㄓㄨˋ	to block the way
25	南來北往	nánláiběiwǎng	ㄋㄢˊ ㄌㄞˊ ㄅㄟˇ ㄨㄤˇ	busy traffic from the south and to the north
26	交通	jiāotōng	ㄐㄧㄠ ㄊㄨㄥ	travel
27	彎路	wānlù	ㄨㄢ ㄌㄨˋ	winding road
28	挖掉	wādiào	ㄨㄚ ㄉㄧㄠˋ	to dig away
29	想法	xiǎngfǎ	ㄒㄧㄤˇ ㄈㄚˇ	idea
30	到底	dàodǐ	ㄉㄠˋ ㄉㄧˇ	in the end
31	只有	zhǐyǒu	ㄓˇ ㄧㄡˇ	only
32	土堆	tǔduī	ㄊㄨˇ ㄉㄨㄟ	pile of dirt
33	搬	bān	ㄅㄢ	to move
34	你一言我一語	nǐyīyánwǒyīyǔ	ㄋㄧˇ ㄧ ㄧㄢˊ ㄨㄛˇ ㄧ ㄩˇ	a lively discussion
35	智	zhì	ㄓˋ	a surname; wisdom
36	只是	zhǐshì	ㄓˇ ㄕˋ	except that; but
37	笑話	xiàohuà	ㄒㄧㄠˋ ㄏㄨㄚˋ	to laugh at
38	子子孫孫	zǐzǐsūnsūn	ㄗˇ ㄗˇ ㄙㄨㄣ ㄙㄨㄣ	sons and grandsons

第十章　铁杵磨针和愚公移山

中国人有句古话说："世上无难事，只怕有心人[1]。"意思是，一个人只要有决心[2]，就没有办[3]不到的事情。因为从古到今有很多的中国人相信这句话，所以，民间[4]就传下来一些故事，让人记住这个道理。当然，有的时候这些故事看起来是很笨的事情。可是，这些故事的意思是为了叫人学习肯下决心，认真作事。下面就是两个这样的故事。

铁[5]杵[6]磨[7]针[8]

中国古时候有一个大诗人，名字叫李白。传说李白小时候不喜欢读书，一天到晚都在外面玩。家里的人都不知道对他该[9]怎麽办[10]。日子[11]就这麽一天一天的过去了。

有一天，李白来到一条河边玩。他突然发现有一位老太太也在河边。老太太正拿著一根铁棒[12]在石头上磨。老太太很用心[13]的在磨，李白走近了，她也不知道。李白觉得很奇怪，就问老太太说："您在作什麽呢？"老太太看也没看李白一眼[14]，继续磨著铁棒。她回答说："我要把它磨成一根针。"

李白听了觉得更奇怪了，又问她说："这麼粗[15]的铁棒，怎麼可能磨成针呢？"老太太说："我今天磨，明天也磨。铁棒只会越磨越细[16]，总有一天[17]它会被我磨成针的。"

李白回家以後天天想著这件事情。他没有办法相信[18]世界上还有这样一位老太太，要把铁棒磨成针。但是他想，如果我们做事情都是这样肯下决心，那还有什麼事情不能做成[19]呢？从这以後[20]，李白就非常用功地学习。後来，他成了一个有名的大诗人。

愚[21]公[22]移[23]山

传说古时候在中国的北方，有两座大山。一座叫太行山，一座叫王屋山。这两座山非常的大，又非常的高。它们挡住[24]了南来北往[25]的去路，使人们的交通[26]和生活很不方便。

有一位老人名叫愚公，年纪已经九十岁了。他的家就是被这两座山挡住了去路。每次愚公和家里的人要去什麼地方，都要走很远的弯路[27]。所以，愚公和家里的人都觉得很不方便。

愚公就把家里的人找来，对他们说："我们一起把这两座山挖掉[28]，这样我们以後就方便了。你们说怎麼样？"大家都觉得这个想法[29]很好。愚叔叔和愚姑姑们也很同意。还有小孙子不愚抢著话说，到底[30]是爷爷年纪大，有办法。我们愚家这麼多人，每天都住在山里真没有什麼意思。挖挖山不是很好玩吗？

只有[31]愚公的妻子觉得不行。愚老太太也差不多九十岁了。她说愚公的一生都是在想一些最笨的事情做。做太太的最知道愚公是一个什麽样的人了。她说："以前你想挖开两个小小的土堆[32]，一直到现在都做不成。怎麽可能去挖走两座那麽大的山呢？即使你真的能挖掉这两座山，那些土和石头又搬[33]到哪里去呢？"

大家觉得愚老太太的话也很有道理，就你一言我一语[34]的谈起来。三愚叔说，土和石头可以搬到海里去，三愚姑说那可能要搬一年的时间。小孙子不愚又抢著话说，不需要搬到海里去。只需要把北边的山挖到西边，南边的山挖到东边就可以了。可是愚公说，以後两座山又会挡住东西方向的去路，再要挖回来就麻烦了。最後大家还是决定把土和石头搬到海里去。

有一个人，姓智[35]。大家都叫他智伯。他是愚公的好朋友，只是[36]两个人总是谈不到一起。他听说愚公不搬家，反而要搬山，觉得世界上有愚公这样的笨人，真是少见。他一定要去跟他谈一谈。他就来到愚公的家，对他说："你已经九十岁了，还能活多久呢？你这样做，不怕天下的人笑话[37]你吗？"

愚公回答说："你怎麽这麽笨？我死了以後，我的儿子还会继续挖。儿子死了，又有孙子。子子孙孙[38]是可以一直挖下去的。这两座山却不会变高，总有一天会被挖平的。"智伯虽然还有很多的问题，可是看到愚公这麽有决心，就不再说话了。後来，这件事感动了天上的神，神就把这两座山搬走了。

阅读理解：

一、 你认为这两个故事想要教我们的是什麽？

二、 智伯後来为什麽不说话了？

三、 李白是谁？

四、 你读过李白的诗吗？

五、 谈谈你对"天下无难事，只怕有心人"的看法。

六、 在你的人生中，你见过老太太或愚公这样的人吗？

生字

1	有心人	yǒuxīnrén	to be resolved
2	决心	juéxīn	perseverance; determination
3	办	bàn	to accomplish
4	民间	mínjiān	folk
5	铁	tiě	iron
6	杵	chǔ	pestle; staff
7	磨	mó	to grind
8	针	zhēn	needle
9	该	gāi	ought to
10	怎麽办	zěmobàn	how to deal with...
11	日子	rìzi	the days
12	棒	bàng	club; staff
13	用心	yòngxīn	concentrated; careful
14	看也没看…一眼	kànyěméikàn…yìyǎn	didn't even glance at

15	粗	cū	thick
16	细	xì	fine; thin
17	总有一天	zǒngyǒuyītiān	someday
18	相信	xiāngxìn	to believe
19	做成	zuòchéng	to accomplish; to succeed
20	从这以後	cóngzhèyǐhòu	from then on
21	愚	yú	foolish
22	公	gōng	Mister
23	移	yí	to move
24	挡住	dǎngzhù	to block the way
25	南来北往	nánláiběiwǎng	busy traffic from the south and to the north
26	交通	jiāotōng	travel
27	弯路	wānlù	winding road
28	挖掉	wādiào	to dig away
29	想法	xiǎngfǎ	idea
30	到底	dàodǐ	in the end
31	只有	zhǐyǒu	only
32	土堆	tǔduī	pile of dirt
33	搬	bān	to move
34	你一言我一语	nǐyīyánwǒyīyǔ	a lively discussion
35	智	zhì	a surname; wisdom
36	只是	zhǐshì	except that; but
37	笑话	xiàohuà	to laugh at
38	子子孙孙	zǐzǐsūnsūn	sons and grandsons

Chapter 10   An Iron Staff Can be Ground Down to a Needle and Yu Gong Moves the Mountain

There is an old Chinese saying: "If people are resolved, there will be no obstacles." The meaning is that with perseverance, a person will be able to accomplish anything. Chinese people have believed in this saying since ancient times, and several stories illustrating this basic truth have been passed down among the people. These stories can seem quite foolish at times, but they are stories which make people want to persevere and do things conscientiously. The following are two such stories.

An Iron Staff Can be Ground Down to a Needle, or Perseverance Will Prevail

In ancient times, there was a great poet called Li Bai. It is said that Li Bai didn't like studying when he was small, instead he liked to play from morning until night. His family didn't know what to do about him and the days passed one after the other.

One day when Li Bai was playing by the river he suddenly saw an old woman nearby. She was grinding an iron staff on a rock. She was so concentrated on grinding that she didn't notice when Li Bai approached. Li Bai was curious and asked, "What are you doing?" The old woman didn't even glance at Li Bai but continued grinding. She answered, "I want to grind it into a needle."

When Li Bai heard this, he thought it very strange and asked, "How could you possibly grind such a thick iron staff into a needle?" The old woman answered, "I will grind today, and I will grind tomorrow. The iron staff can only become thinner and one day it will be ground down to a needle."

After Li Bai got home, he thought about what he had seen. He couldn't believe that someone like this still existed in this world, an old woman who wanted to grind an iron staff into a needle. He began to think that if we were all as willing to persevere in our endeavors, we could accomplish anything. From that day on, Li Bai began to study diligently and, in the end, he became one of China's great and famous poets.

Yu Gong Moves the Mountain

In ancient times, it is said that there were two large mountains in the north of China. One was called Tai Hang Mountain and the other was called Wang Wu Mountain. These two mountains were both very big and very tall and they blocked the passage from north to south. This made life and travel very difficult for the people.

There was an old man called Yu Gong who was ninety-years-old. The way to his house was blocked by the two mountains. Whenever Yu Gong and his family wanted to go somewhere, they had to take a very long, winding road to get there. They all felt that it was most inconvenient.

So Yu Gong called together his whole family and said, "Let us dig these two mountains away. It would be much more convenient for us, what do you think?" They all thought it was a good idea. Uncle Yu and Aunt Yu also agreed. Even the grandson Bu Yu chimed in and said that grandpa was elderly and had experience in these things. "Our whole family up in the mountains with nothing to do all day is boring, so I think digging up the mountain will be fun," he said.

Only Yu Gong's wife was opposed to the idea. Mrs. Yu was also almost ninety-years-old. She said that throughout Yu Gong's life he had always thought of doing the most foolish things. Being his wife, she knew Yu Gong best of all. She said, "One time in the past you wanted to remove two tiny dirt piles, you still haven't finished doing that. How would you ever manage to dig away two large mountains? And even if you did manage to do it, where would you put all the dirt and rocks?"

When the family heard what Mrs. Yu had to say, they thought that she too was right and a lively discussion followed. Third Uncle Yu said that they could bring the dirt and the rocks to the sea. Third Aunt Yu said that that would take a whole year to accomplish, but Bu Yu piped in that the dirt and rocks needn't be carried to the sea, instead the northern mountain could be moved to the west and the southern mountain could be moved to the east. But Yu Gong countered that by doing it that way, the path going east-west would be blocked and they would have to start digging again, which would be a nuisance. Finally they all agreed that the dirt and rocks would have to be brought to the sea.

There was a man called Zhi whom everybody called Uncle Zhi. He was Yu Gong's good friend, but the two never could agree on anything. When he heard that Yu Gong was planning to move the mountain instead of moving his house, he thought that he had never heard of anyone so stupid. So he decided he had to go speak to Yu Gong. When he arrived at Yu Gong's house, he said, "You are already ninety-years-old, how much longer do you think you'll live? Aren't you afraid that everyone will laugh at you for doing this?"

Yu Gong answered, "How can you be so stupid? After I die, my sons will continue to dig, and after they die, my grandsons will. Sons and grandsons will always continue to dig. These two mountains will definitely not get any taller, some day they will be flat." Although Uncle Zhi still had many questions, he saw how determined Yu Gong was and said no more. God up in the heavens was so moved by this story that he took the two mountains away.

第十一章　岳飛大將和蘇武牧羊

蘇武牧羊

　　岳飛[1]是宋朝[2]的一位大將[3]。那時候，天下很不平安，到處是打仗。宋朝被從北方來的外國人搶走了一半的中國土地，而且把皇帝也搶走了。後來，新接上來[4]的皇帝就在中國的南方找人民來打仗。皇帝這時很怕打仗，可是他又希望收回[5]另一半的中國。這時，皇帝就找到了岳飛，他是一位非常有天才和能力的人。

傳說，岳飛很小的時候，他的家附近了發生大水。大水使他的家裏所有的東西都沒有了。岳飛和母親坐在一口缸裏[6]，所以，他們才沒有在大水裏死去。後來，岳飛的爸爸去世了，岳飛就跟著母親讀了很多的書。

當皇帝開始在找人打仗的時候，岳飛的母親對兒子說："現在是你為國家服務的時候了。你應該把自己完全交給[7]國家。"岳飛聽了很難過，因為他的母親已經老了。其實她很需要有兒子在身邊，幫助她每天的生活。可是，母親為了國家，卻可以不管自己的需要了。

為了讓岳飛不忘記為國家服務，岳飛的母親在他的背上刺[8]了四個大字："盡忠報國[9]"。岳飛一直記住母親的話和她的希望。因為岳飛很有能力，所以他幫助皇帝收回了很多的土地。因為他的能力很大，所以北方的外國人一聽說岳飛來了，就很怕他。

後來，北方的外國人想了一個辦法，用錢買下了皇帝手下[10]的一個人，這個人就把岳飛給殺了。岳飛死的時候，為國家服務的心一點也沒有變，他那時只有三十九歲。

蘇武牧[11]羊[12]

　　蘇武是中國漢朝時候的人。那時候，中國北方有一個國家，這個國家叫匈奴[13]國。匈奴國常常來打中國，使中國的人民不能平安地生活。皇帝特別喜歡蘇武，就讓他帶一百人代表皇帝去匈奴國，送給他們許多禮物。希望兩國不要打仗，成爲朋友。

　　可是，匈奴國的皇帝覺得中國送禮物來，是因爲害怕[14]，沒有能力和匈奴國打仗。他們把蘇武關[15]起來，用很多的方法，想要讓蘇武給匈奴國服務，但蘇武一點也不變心[16]。匈奴人把他放在雪地裏，不給他東西吃，也不讓他和手下人在一起。幾天後，匈奴皇帝看見蘇武沒有死，也沒有變心，就很喜歡他。可是，他們仍然沒有辦法使蘇武爲匈奴國服務。

　　匈奴皇帝就把他放到北海的一個沒有人住的地方，給了蘇武幾隻公羊[17]，對他說：“等公羊生了小羊，我們就放你回中國去。”蘇武在北海放羊[18]，放了十九年。身邊沒有一個人，生活非常的難，而且還常常沒有東西吃。

　　最後，匈奴皇帝還是把蘇武放回了中國。蘇武回到中國，中國的皇帝已經死了。蘇武的太太也跟他離婚[19]了。蘇武離開中國到匈奴的時候是四十歲，現在已經是一個白髮老人[20]了。他離開中國的時候，帶去的有一百人，回來的時候只有九個人。但是，所有的事情都變了，只有蘇武的心沒有變，蘇武的故事影響了後來的很多人。

閱讀理解：

一、　誰是岳飛？

二、　爲什麼岳飛會被皇帝殺了？

三、　你認爲岳飛的母親教育孩子的方法對嗎？

四、　蘇武代表中國去北方做什麼？

五、　蘇武爲什麼這麼愛中國而不變心？

六、　岳飛和蘇武的故事，告訴我們什麼道理？

七、　你認爲岳飛和蘇武這樣的人，在現代是不是還適用？

生字

[1] 岳飛	yuèfēi	ㄩㄝˋ ㄈㄟ	*name of a general of the Song Dynasty*
[2] 宋朝	sòngcháo	ㄙㄨㄥˋ ㄔㄠˊ	*Song Dynasty*
[3] 大將	dàjiàng	ㄉㄚˋ ㄐㄧㄤˋ	*general*
[4] 接上來	jiēshànglái	ㄐㄧㄝ ㄕㄤˋ ㄌㄞˊ	*to take over*
[5] 收回	shōuhuí	ㄕㄡ ㄏㄨㄟˊ	*to recover*
[6] 缸里	gānglǐ	ㄍㄤ ㄌㄧˇ	*earthen jar*
[7] 交給	jiāogěi	ㄐㄧㄠ ㄍㄟˇ	*to give oneself to...*
[8] 刺	cì	ㄘˋ	*to etch; to engrave*
[9] 盡忠報國	jìnzhōng bàoguó	ㄐㄧㄣˋ ㄓㄨㄥ ㄅㄠˋ ㄍㄨㄛˊ	*Use all your loyalty to serve your country*
[10] 手下	shǒuxià	ㄕㄡˇ ㄒㄧㄚˋ	*under the leadership*
[11] 牧	mù	ㄇㄨˋ	*to tend*
[12] 羊	yáng	ㄧㄤˊ	*sheep*

¹³ 匈奴	xiōngnú	ㄒㄩㄥ ㄋㄨˊ	name of a nomadic tribe (Hun)
¹⁴ 害怕	hàipà	ㄏㄞˋ ㄆㄚˋ	to be afraid
¹⁵ 關	guān	ㄍㄨㄢ	to lock up
¹⁶ 變心	biànxīn	ㄅㄧㄢˋ ㄒㄧㄣ	to become unfaithful
¹⁷ 公羊	gōngyáng	ㄍㄨㄥ ㄧㄤˊ	ram
¹⁸ 放羊	fàngyáng	ㄈㄤˋ ㄧㄤˊ	to herd sheep
¹⁹ 離婚	líhūn	ㄌㄧˊ ㄏㄨㄣ	to divorce
²⁰ 白髮老人	báifàlǎorén	ㄅㄞˊ ㄈㄚˋ ㄌㄠˇ ㄖㄣˊ	an old person with white hair

第十一章　岳飞大将和苏武牧羊

　　岳飞[1]是宋朝[2]的一位大将[3]。那时候，天下很不平安，到处是打仗。宋朝被从北方来的外国人抢走了一半的中国土地，而且把皇帝也抢走了。後来，新接上来[4]的皇帝就在中国的南方找人民来打仗。皇帝这时很怕打仗，可是他又希望收回[5]另一半的中国。这时，皇帝就找到了岳飞，他是一位非常有天才和能力的人。

　　传说，岳飞很小的时候，他的家附近了发生大水。大水使他的家里所有的东西都没有了。岳飞和母亲坐在一口缸里[6]，所以，他们才没有在大水里死去。後来，岳飞的爸爸去世了，岳飞就跟著母亲读了很多的书。

　　当皇帝开始在找人打仗的时候，岳飞的母亲对儿子说："现在是你为国家服务的时候了。你应该把自己完全交给[7]国家。"岳飞听了很难过，因为他的母亲已经老了。其实她很需要有儿子在身边，帮助她每天的生活。可是，母亲为了国家，却可以不管自己的需要了。

为了让岳飞不忘记为国家服务，岳飞的母亲在他的背上刺[8]了四个大字："尽忠报国[9]"。岳飞一直记住母亲的话和她的希望。因为岳飞很有能力，所以他帮助皇帝收回了很多的土地。因为他的能力很大，所以北方的外国人一听说岳飞来了，就很怕他。

後来，北方的外国人想了一个办法，用钱买下了皇帝手下[10]的一个人，这个人就把岳飞给杀了。岳飞死的时候，为国家服务的心一点也没有变，他那时只有三十九岁。

苏武牧[11]羊[12]

苏武是中国汉朝时候的人。那时候，中国北方有一个国家，这个国家叫匈奴[13]国。匈奴国常常来打中国，使中国的人民不能平安地生活。皇帝特别喜欢苏武，就让他带一百人代表皇帝去匈奴国，送给他们许多礼物。希望两国不要打仗，成为朋友。

可是，匈奴国的皇帝觉得中国送礼物来，是因为害怕[14]，没有能力和匈奴国打仗。他们把苏武关[15]起来，用很多的方法，想要让苏武给匈奴国服务，但苏武一点也不变心[16]。匈奴人把他放在雪地里，不给他东西吃，也不让他和手下人在一起。几天後，匈奴皇帝看见苏武没有死，也没有变心，就很喜欢他。可是，他们仍然没有办法使苏武为匈奴国服务。

匈奴皇帝就把他放到北海的一个没有人住的地方，给了苏武几只公羊[17]，对他说："等公羊生了小羊，我们就放你回中国去。"苏武在北海放羊[18]，放了十九年。身边没有一个人，生活非常的难，而且还常常没有东西吃。

最後，匈奴皇帝还是把苏武放回了中国。苏武回到中国，中国的皇帝已经死了。苏武的太太也跟他离婚[19]了。苏武离开中国到匈奴的时候是四十岁，现在已经是一个白发老人[20]了。他离开中国的时候，带去的有一百人，回来的时候只有九个人。但是，所有的事情都变了，只有苏武的心没有变，苏武的故事影响了後来的很多人。

阅读理解：

一、　谁是岳飞？

二、　为什麽岳飞会被皇帝杀了？

三、　你认为岳飞的母亲教育孩子的方法对吗？

四、　苏武代表中国去北方做什麽？

五、　苏武为什麽这麽爱中国而不变心？

六、　岳飞和苏武的故事，告诉我们什麽道理？

七、　你认为岳飞和苏武这样的人，在现代是不是还适用？

生字

1	岳飞	yuèfēi	name of a general of the Song Dynasty
2	宋朝	sòngcháo	Song Dynasty
3	大将	dàjiàng	general
4	接上来	jiēshànglái	to take over
5	收回	shōuhuí	to recover
6	缸里	gānglǐ	earthen jar
7	交给	jiāogěi	to give oneself to...
8	刺	cì	to etch; to engrave
9	尽忠报国	jìnzhōngbàoguó	Use all your loyalty to serve your country
10	手下	shǒuxià	under the leadership
11	牧	mù	to tend
12	羊	yáng	sheep
13	匈奴	xiōngnú	name of a nomadic tribe (Hun)
14	害怕	hàipà	to be afraid
15	关	guān	to lock up
16	变心	biànxīn	to become unfaithful
17	公羊	gōngyáng	ram
18	放羊	fàngyáng	to herd sheep
19	离婚	líhūn	to divorce
20	白发老人	báifàlǎorén	an old person with white hair

Chapter 11   General Yue Fei and Su Wu Herds Sheep

Yue Fei was a great general of the Song Dynasty. It was not a peaceful time and there were wars everywhere. During the Song Dynasty, half of the Chinese territory had been invaded by foreigners from the north. The new emperor brought people from the south of China to fight in the wars. The emperor was afraid of war but he did want to recover the other half of China. Then the emperor found Yue Fei, who was an extremely talented and able man.

The story goes that there was a flood near Yue Fei's house when he was a child. His family lost everything they owned in that flood. Yue Fei and his mother sat inside a large earthen jar and were able to save their lives. Later, when Yue Fei's father died, Yue Fei emulated his mother and read many books.

At the time when the emperor was looking for people to fight in the war, Yue Fei's mother said to her son, "The time for you to serve your country has come. You must give yourself entirely to your country." Yue Fei was upset when he heard this. His mother was old and needed him to be near her to help her with her daily life. But his mother, for the sake of the country, ignored her personal needs.

To help him remember to serve his country, Yue Fei's mother etched four large words on his back that said: "Use all your loyalty to serve the country." Yue Fei always remembered his mother's words and her hopes. Because of his great ability, Yue Fei was able to help the emperor win back a lot of China's territory. Because of Yue Fei's great ability, the northern invaders felt afraid whenever they heard his name.

Later on, the northerners thought of an idea. They offered money to one of the emperor's men to kill Yue Fei. When he died, Yue Fei's devotion to his country had not changed. He was only thirty-nine-years-old.

Su Wu Tends the Sheep

Su Wu lived during China's Han Dynasty. At that time, there was a tribe living north of China called the Xiong Nu (Hun). The Xiong Nu often attacked China, and the people of China could not live in peace. The emperor, who was very fond of Su Wu, sent Su Wu as his representative to the Xiong Nu, taking one hundred men and some gifts. The emperor hoped that the two territories would stop fighting and become friends.

The emperor of the Xiong Nu Tribe, on the other hand, believed that the gifts were a sign that China was afraid and incapable of fighting the Xiong Nu. He locked Su Wu up and tried all sorts of methods to force Su Wu to serve the country of the Xiong Nu. But Su Wu never ceased to be faithful to his own country. The Xiong Nu people placed him in the snow to let him starve, separating Su Wu from his people. After several days, when the emperor of the Xiong Nu saw that Su Wu had not died nor ceased to be faithful, he admired him greatly. But still he could not make Su Wu serve the country of Xiong Nu.

The emperor of the Xiong Nu had Su Wu banished to an area near the North Sea where no other people lived. He also sent some rams along with Su Wu and said, "Wait until those rams give birth to lambs and we will let you go back to China." So Su Wu herded sheep at the North Sea; he herded for nineteen years. He was completely alone, life was extremely difficult, and he often had nothing to eat.

In the end, the emperor of the Xiong Nu allowed Su Wu to return to China. When he got there, the emperor of China had already died and Su Wu's wife had divorced him. When Su Wu left China to go to the Xiong Nu he was forty-years-old, now he was an old man with white hair. When he left China he took one hundred men with him, when he returned home he had only nine with him. Even though everything had changed around him, Su Wu's heart had not changed. This story of Su Wu influenced many later generations.

第十二章　本草綱目和神醫華陀

本草綱目

　　上古的時候，人們的生活都很簡單。人們所吃的東西，都是從大自然裏來的。可是，因爲不知道什麼東西可以吃，什麼東西不可以吃，就生了許多的病。有的時候，人們會因爲吃錯了東西而生病或死去。所以，在古時候的中國，傳說有一個叫神農¹的人。他爲了使別人不再生病或者死去，就自己試著吃每一種大自然裏的東西。然後，他就把經驗告訴別人。人們就不會再因吃了不好的東西而死去了。可是,這是傳說裏的故事。在中國歷史上,真的有人爲了別人的病去吃大自然裏的草。李時珍[2]和華陀就是這樣的人。

李時珍是明朝[3]的一位醫學家[4]。他的父親和祖父[5]都是中醫[6]的醫生[7]。李時珍小的時候,常常看父親給病人醫病。他看到父親用草藥[8]救活[9]了許多的人。他希望自己長大以後,也能做醫生,給病人看病。可是,李時珍的父親卻不喜歡他做醫生。

那時候,醫生是被人看不起[10]的。所以,醫生的生活也是很不容易的。醫生給人看病,收的錢非常的少。李時珍常常看見父親給人看病不收錢,因爲那時候很多人沒有錢。可是,李時珍卻決心做醫生。他常常站在父親的後面,看父親給病人醫病。有一次,父親遇見一個很難的病,不知道應該怎樣做。這時,李時珍就說出了一種藥的名字。父親一聽,覺得很對,那個病人就被醫好了。從那以後,父親就同意他學醫。二十二歲的時候,李時珍就開始給人看病了。

李時珍一邊給病人看病,一邊研究藥。他發現有很多的藥,都是書上沒有的。書上的藥很多也寫得不對。他想,如果藥書寫錯了,病人可能會吃錯了藥,那將是一件很可怕[11]的事。所以,李時珍就決心寫一部新的中藥書。

爲了寫這本中藥書,李時珍就在醫病的時候,注意把經驗記下來。他還到高山上去找各種的藥。對很多的新藥,李時珍都自己先吃，看看藥怎麼樣。他還訪問了許多的農民、醫生、和獵人，學到了很多書上沒有記下來的東西。最後，李時珍回到家裏，開始寫書。他整整花了二十七年的時間，才寫完這部書。這部中藥書的名字叫"本草綱目[12]"。它有一百多萬字，記下了一千八百多種藥。現在這本書已經流傳到了世界上許多的國家。

神醫[13]華陀[14]

華陀生在三國時代。那時候，中國到處都在打仗。因為打仗和生活不平安，所以那時候就有很多的病人。華陀決定去學醫，慢慢的，華陀就成了一位名醫。華陀原來有一個當皇帝的醫生的機會，可以過很好的生活。可是，他覺得太多的人需要醫生，所以他還是決定為人民服務。

有一次，華陀上山找藥，遇見了一隻受傷[15]的小鹿[16]。他看到了很難過，要去醫小鹿的傷。他就跟在小鹿後面走，一直走到一個長滿草的水邊。小鹿來到水邊，喝了幾口水，就倒下了。華陀以為小鹿死了，走過去才發現小鹿是睡著[17]了。華陀想，如果喝了這種水，病人就可以睡著，那不是可以給病人開刀[18]了嗎？華陀就發現水邊有一種草，吃了可以使人睡著。他就發明了一種麻藥[19]，是為病人做外科[20]手術[21]用的。病人喝了以後就睡著了，起來的時候，手術已經做完了。結果，華陀就做了世界上第一個外科手術，離現在有一千七百多年。

　　華陀覺得，鍛鍊[22]身體[23]比醫病更重要。所以他就發明了一種鍛鍊身體的方法。這種方法是學許多動物的動作[24]。用這種方法每天鍛鍊身體，人就不容易生病。後來，這種方法成爲中國功夫[25]的起源[26]，而且現在中醫用的針灸[27]方法也是從華陀開始的。

　　那時候，曹操還是一個國家的國王。他聽說華陀這個人很有能力，就要他來給自己看病。曹操的頭有很重的病，第一次華陀就給他醫好了。曹操就問華陀說，有什麼辦法可以使我的頭永遠不再有病？華陀告訴曹操，只有一個辦法，就是把他的頭打開[28]。這樣才能把病都拿走。

　　曹操一聽，就很生氣，以爲是華陀要殺他。曹操就把華陀關起來了。華陀在被關的時候，把自己許多年來做醫生的經驗寫下來，讓他的學生把這些經驗傳給後人。不久，曹操就把華陀殺了。

閱讀理解：

一、　誰是神農？

二、　李時珍是誰？

三、　李時珍是怎樣開始行醫的？

四、　李時珍對中醫有什麼影響？

五、　華陀是怎樣發現麻藥的？

六、　中國功夫是怎樣來的？

七、　華陀是怎樣死的？他對中國醫學有什麼影響？

八、　你有沒有試過針炙？

九、　談談你對中醫和西醫的看法。

生字

¹ 神農	shénnóng	ㄕㄣˊ ㄋㄨㄥˊ	*name of a legendary man*
² 李時珍	lǐshízhēn	ㄌㄧˇ ㄕˊ ㄓㄣ	*name of an historical medical scholar*
³ 明朝	míngcháo	ㄇㄧㄥˊ ㄔㄠˊ	*Ming Dynasty*
⁴ 醫學家	yīxuéjiā	ㄧ ㄒㄩㄝˊ ㄐㄧㄚ	*medical scholar*
⁵ 祖父	zǔfù	ㄗㄨˇ ㄈㄨˋ	*grandfather*
⁶ 中醫	zhōngyī	ㄓㄨㄥ ㄧ	*Chinese medicine*
⁷ 醫生	yīshēng	ㄧ ㄕㄥ	*doctor*
⁸ 草藥	cǎoyào	ㄘㄠˇ ㄧㄠˋ	*herbal medicine*
⁹ 救活	jiùhuó	ㄐㄧㄡˋ ㄏㄨㄛˊ	*to save lives*

10	看不起	kànbùqǐ	ㄎㄢˋ ㄅㄨˋ ㄑㄧˇ	to look down on
11	可怕	kěpà	ㄎㄜˇ ㄆㄚˋ	terrible; frightening
12	本草綱目	běncǎogāngmù	ㄅㄣˇ ㄘㄠˇ ㄍㄤ ㄇㄨˋ	"The Compendium of Materia Medica"
13	神醫	shényī	ㄕㄣˊ ㄧ	a miracle worker
14	華陀	huàtuó	ㄏㄨㄚˋ ㄊㄨㄛˊ	name of a famous doctor
15	受傷	shòushāng	ㄕㄡˋ ㄕㄤ	injured
16	小鹿	xiǎolù	ㄒㄧㄠˇ ㄌㄨˋ	fawn
17	睡著	shuìzháo	ㄕㄨㄟˋ ㄓㄠˊ	to sleep
18	開刀	kāidāo	ㄎㄞ ㄅㄠ	to perform an operation; surgery
19	麻藥	máyào	ㄇㄚˊ ㄧㄠˋ	anesthetic
20	外科	wàikē	ㄨㄞˋ ㄎㄜ	surgical
21	手術	shǒushù	ㄕㄡˇ ㄕㄨˋ	operation
22	鍛煉	duànliàn	ㄅㄨㄢˋ ㄌㄧㄢˋ	physical exercise
23	身體	shēntǐ	ㄕㄣ ㄊㄧˇ	the body
24	動作	dòngzuò	ㄅㄨㄥˋ ㄗㄨㄛˋ	movement
25	功夫	gōngfū	ㄍㄨㄥ ㄈㄨ	Kung Fu
26	起源	qǐyuán	ㄑㄧˇ ㄩㄢˊ	origin
27	針灸	zhēnjiǔ	ㄓㄣ ㄐㄧㄡˇ	acupuncture and moxibustion
28	打開	dǎkāi	ㄅㄚˇ ㄎㄞ	to open

第十二章　本草纲目和神医华陀

上古的时候，人们的生活都很简单。人们所吃的东西，都是从大自然里来的。可是，因为不知道什麼东西可以吃，什麼东西不可以吃，就生了许多的病。有的时候，人们会因为吃错了东西而生病或死去。所以，在古时候的中国，传说有一个叫神农[1]的人。他为了使别人不再生病或者死去，就自己试著吃每一种大自然里的东西。然後，他就把经验告诉别人。人们就不会再因吃了不好的东西而死去了。可是，这是传说里的故事。在中国历史上，真的有人为了别人的病去吃大自然里的草。李时珍[2]和华陀就是这样的人。

李时珍是明朝[3]的一位医学家[4]。他的父亲和祖父[5]都是中医[6]的医生[7]。李时珍小的时候，常常看父亲给病人医病。他看到父亲用草药[8]救活[9]了许多的人。他希望自己长大以後，也能做医生，给病人看病。可是，李时珍的父亲却不喜欢他做医生。

那时候，医生是被人看不起[10]的。所以，医生的生活也是很不容易的。医生给人看病，收的钱非常的少。李时珍常常看见父亲给人看病不收钱，因为那时候很多人没有钱。可是，李时珍却决心做医生。他常常站在父亲的後面，看父亲给病人医病。有一次，父亲遇见一个很难的病，不知道应该怎样做。这时，李时珍就说出了一种药的名字。父亲一听，觉得很对，那个病人就被医好了。从那以後，父亲就同意他学医。二十二岁的时候，李时珍就开始给人看病了。

李时珍一边给病人看病，一边研究药。他发现有很多的药，都是书上没有的。书上的药很多也写得不对。他想，如果药书写错了，病人可能会吃错了药，那将是一件很可怕[11]的事。所以，李时珍就决心写一部新的中药书。

为了写这本中药书，李时珍就在医病的时候，注意把经验记下来。他还到高山上去找各种的药。对很多的新药，李时珍都自己先吃，看看药怎麽样。他还访问了许多的农民、医生、和猎人，学到了很多书上没有记下来的东西。最后，李时珍回到家里，开始写书。他整整花了二十七年的时间，才写完这部书。这部中药书的名字叫"本草纲目[12]"。它有一百多万字，记下了一千八百多种药。现在这本书已经流传到了世界上许多的国家。

神医[13]华陀[14]

华陀生在三国时代。那时候，中国到处都在打仗。因为打仗和生活不平安，所以那时候就有很多的病人。华陀决定去学医，慢慢的，华陀就成了一位名医。华陀原来有一个当皇帝的医生的机会，可以过很好的生活。可是，他觉得太多的人需要医生，所以他还是决定为人民服务。

有一次，华陀上山找药，遇见了一只受伤[15]的小鹿[16]。他看到了很难过，要去医小鹿的伤。他就跟在小鹿後面走，一直走到一个长满草的水边。小鹿来到水边，喝了几口水，就倒下了。华陀以为小鹿死了，走过去才发现小鹿是睡著[17]了。华陀想，如果喝了这种水，病人就可以睡著，那不是可以给病人开刀[18]了吗？华陀就发现水边有一种草，吃了可以使人睡著。他就发明了一种麻药[19]，是为病人做外科[20]手术[21]用的。病人喝了以後就睡著了，起来的时候，手术已经做完了。结果，华陀就做了世界上第一个外科手术，离现在有一千七百多年。

华陀觉得，锻炼[22]身体[23]比医病更重要。所以他就发明了一种锻炼身体的方法。这种方法是学许多动物的动作[24]。用这种方法每天锻炼身体，人就不容易生病。後来，这种方法成为中国功夫[25]的起源[26]，而且现在中医用的针灸[27]方法也是从华陀开始的。

那时候，曹操还是一个国家的国王。他听说华陀这个人很有能力，就要他来给自己看病。曹操的头有很重的病，第一次华陀就给他医好了。曹操就问华陀说，有什麽办法可以使我的头永远不再有病？华陀告诉曹操，只有一个办法，就是把他的头打开[28]。这样才能把病都拿走。

曹操一听，就很生气，以为是华陀要杀他。曹操就把华陀关起来了。华陀在被关的时候，把自己许多年来做医生的经验写下来，让他的学生把这些经验传给後人。不久，曹操就把华陀杀了。

阅读理解：

一、 谁是神农？

二、 李时珍是谁？

三、 李时珍是怎样开始行医的？

四、 李时珍对中医有什麽影响？

五、 华陀是怎样发现麻药的？

六、 中国功夫是怎样来的？

七、 华陀是怎样死的？他对中国医学有什麽影响？

八、 你有没有试过针炙？

九、 谈谈你对中医和西医的看法。

生字

1	神农	shénnóng	name of a legendary man
2	李时珍	lǐshízhēn	name of an historical medical scholar
3	明朝	míngcháo	Ming Dynasty
4	医学家	yīxuéjiā	medical scholar
5	祖父	zǔfù	grandfather
6	中医	zhōngyī	Chinese medicine
7	医生	yīshēng	doctor
8	草药	cǎoyào	herbal medicine
9	救活	jiùhuó	to save lives
10	看不起	kànbùqǐ	to look down on
11	可怕	kěpà	terrible; frightening
12	本草纲目	běncǎogāngmù	"The Compendium of Materia Medica"
13	神医	shényī	a miracle worker
14	华陀	huàtuó	name of a famous doctor
15	受伤	shòushāng	injured
16	小鹿	xiǎolù	fawn
17	睡著	shuìzháo	to sleep
18	开刀	kāidāo	to perform an operation; surgery
19	麻药	máyào	anesthetic
20	外科	wàikē	surgical
21	手术	shǒushù	operation
22	锻炼	duànliàn	physical exercise
23	身体	shēntǐ	the body
24	动作	dòngzuò	movement
25	功夫	gōngfū	Kung Fu
26	起源	qǐyuán	origin
27	针灸	zhēnjiǔ	acupuncture and moxibustion
28	打开	dǎkāi	to open

Chapter 12   The Compendium of Materia Medica and Hua Tuo the Miracle Worker

In early times, life was very simple. The food people ate came from nature. However, the people didn't know the difference between edible and inedible things, so illnesses erupted. Sometimes people ate something by mistake and got ill, or died.

It is said that in ancient China there lived a man called Shen Nong. This man wanted to keep people from getting sick or dying, so he himself tried to eat everything growing in nature. After that, he described his experience to others and the people no longer died from eating something bad. This, however, is a legend. There are also historical figures who actually tried many plants growing outside in order to help people with their illnesses. Li Shi Zhen and Hua Tuo were two such people.

Li Shi Zhen was a medical scholar during the Ming Dynasty. His father and his grandfather had both been doctors of Chinese medicine. When he was a child, Li Shi Zhen had often watched his father give medical treatments to his patients. He had seen his father saving people's lives with herbal medicine. He also wanted to grow up to be a doctor and treat patients. But Li Shi Zhen's father did not want him to become a doctor.

In those days, doctors were not well thought of. The life of a doctor was not very easy. The payments for treatments were very low. Li Shi Zhen saw how frequently his father gave free treatments because everybody was poor in those days. But Li Shi Zhen was determined to be a doctor. He often stood behind his father, watching him give medical treatments. One day his father encountered a man who was suffering from an illness which was difficult to cure. His father didn't know how to help the patient. Suddenly Li Shi Zhen suggested the name of an herb. As soon as his father heard the name, he knew it was the correct remedy. The patient was cured and from then on his father agreed that Li Shi Zhen could become a doctor. Li Shi Zhen started seeing patients when he was twenty-two-years-old.

Li Shi Zhen gave medical treatments and at the same time, he researched medicinal herbs. He discovered many herbs which had not yet been written up in books. Many of the medicinal herbs in the books were not properly described. He thought that it would be a terrible thing if patients took the wrong medicine because the medical books had mistakes in them. For this reason, Li Shi Zhen decided to write a new book about Chinese herbal medicine.

In order to write the Chinese herbal medicine book, Li Shi Zhen carefully recorded all of his experiences while giving medical treatments. He also climbed high up into the mountains to find different kinds of herbs. When he discovered new herbs, he tried them himself to see what the herb was like. He also interviewed many peasants, doctors, and hunters from whom he learned many things that had not been recorded in the books. Finally, Li Shi Zhen returned home and started writing. He spent the whole of twenty-seven years before finishing his book. The title of the book is The Compendium of Materia Medica. It has several million words in it and describes more than 1,800 medicinal herbs. The use of this book has spread to many countries.

Hua Tuo the Miracle Worker

Hua Tuo lived during the Three Kingdoms Period. At that time, there were many wars everywhere in China. Because of the wars and the turbulent times, there were many patients. That is why Hua Tuo decided to study medicine. Slowly but surely, as Hua Tuo gave patients medical treatments, he observed everything carefully and became a famous doctor. At one point he was offered the chance to be the emperor's doctor. He would have had a very comfortable life, but because there were so many people who needed a doctor, he chose to help the people.

One day, when Hua Tuo was up in the mountains collecting herbs, he encountered an injured fawn. It seemed to be suffering and he wanted to look at its injury. He followed the fawn all the way to a watering place surrounded by tall grass. The fawn went up to the water, drank a few mouthfuls of water and fell over. Hua Tuo thought that the fawn had died, but when he approached it, he realized that it was asleep. Hua Tuo thought, if this water makes one go to sleep, couldn't it be used when performing an operation? Then Hua Tuo discovered an herb growing next to the water: it was an herb which put you to sleep if you ate it. From the herb, Hua Tuo invented a kind of anesthetic which could be used for surgical operations. A patient could take the medicine and go to sleep, and when he woke up, the operation would already be over. Therefore, Hua Tuo was the first person on earth to perform a surgical operation. That was 1,700 years ago.

Hua Tuo believed that physical exercise was more important than treating disease, so he developed a method of physical exercise. This method imitated the movements of animals. When people practiced this method of physical exercise everyday, they rarely got sick. These exercises were the origin of Chinese Kung Fu. Chinese acupuncture as we know it today was also begun by Hua Tuo.

At that time, Cao Cao was still the king of one of the countries. When he heard about Hua Tuo's great talent, he wanted Hua Tuo to come and treat him. Cao Cao was suffering from a serious "illness of his head." The first time Hua Tuo treated him, the king was cured.

Cao Cao then asked Hua Tuo how he could ensure that the illness in his head would never return. Hua Tuo answered that the only way to do this would be to open up his head and take the sick part out. Cao Cao was very angry when he heard this. He thought Hua Tuo intended to kill him, so Hua Tuo locked him up. During his imprisonment, Hua Tuo recorded all of his many years of medical experience. He wanted his students to pass on his knowledge to later generations. Soon after, Cao Cao had Hua Tuo killed.

第十三章　太公釣魚和三藏取經

太公釣魚

　　大約在三千多年前，有一個很有才能的人。他曾幫助一個國王建立了一個持續八百年的朝代。這個人姓姜[1]，名字叫太公[2]。別人都叫他姜太公。姜太公雖然很有才能，可是他一生的機會都不好。一直到晚年的時候，他的生活才有了很大的變化。

傳說，姜太公到了五十歲，還沒有做成什麼事。他太太就離開他了。到了六十歲，他還在給別人賣牛肉[3]。七十歲的時候，他又賣起飯來。他的生活非常不好，就是自己一個人的吃和住，都成了問題。可是，姜太公一點也不會不高興。他不覺得自己是一個無用的人，反而告訴別人，自己是一個很有用的人。

最後，姜太公來到一個小河邊，開始釣起魚來。人們不知道他是不是真的要釣魚[4]，因為他釣魚的方法非常特別。他用的魚鉤[5]是直的，也不用魚餌[6]。而且，他的魚鉤是離開水面[7]三尺[8]以上，而不是在水中。所有的人看了，都說這種方法是不可能釣到魚的。

但是，姜太公告訴人們，他真正要釣的不是魚，而是一個機會。他要釣的是一個國王，他的意思是說，將有一個國王會來找他，請他為國王服務。這是他一生的機會。這個機會可以讓他把他一生的才能都用出來。

這個機會終於來了。有一天，一個國王和他手下的人經過這個河邊，發現了姜太公。國王非常喜歡太公的才能，可以幫助國王打仗，太公就成了皇宮裏最重要的人之一。太公幫助國王打了很多仗，最後打敗了另外一個大的國家。

三藏⁹取¹⁰經¹¹

三藏是唐朝¹²時候的一位和尚¹³。他在中國歷史上是非常有名的，因為他離開中國十七年，一個人去印度¹⁴學習佛經¹⁵，然後把佛教¹⁶帶回到中國。他帶回來的佛經有一千三百三十五本，並且把它們都翻譯¹⁷成了中文。

三藏從小就出家¹⁸做了和尚。他非常喜歡讀佛經，才二十多歲，就把他能找到的佛經都讀完了。可是，他發現在中國，佛經很不完全。而且，三藏有很多的問題，也沒有人能給他滿意的回答。所以，三藏就決定自己去西方印度，在那裏學習佛經和佛教的道理¹⁹。

那時候，交通很不方便，路又遠，什麼事情都可能發生。可是，三藏因為有很大的決心²⁰，不怕所有可能發生的事情，他一個人離開了中國。那時，三藏才二十六歲。一路上，他經過了許多的高山和沙漠²¹。最後他來到了印度。在印度，三藏學習了五年的佛學道理和許多古代的學問，在印度他是一個很有名的和尚。

三藏的名字被很多的國家和國王知道了，他們都希望能和他見面。三藏這時開始旅行，他一共走了五十六個國家，見到了許多的國王。他曾在七、八千人和十八個國王的前面，向大家談佛教的道理。從那以後，三藏的名字就被更多的人知道了。這時，中國的皇帝才知道有一位和尚在印度很出名。

　　三藏回來時，他已經四十三歲了。他得到了皇帝的幫助，把帶回來的佛經都翻譯成了中文。他又寫了一些書，把他去印度，一路上所看見的事情都告訴了人們。這本書後來被寫成了小說[22]。三藏的一生，使佛教對中國文化有了很大的影響。

閱讀理解

一、　姜太公是誰？

二、　姜太公和愚公有什麼地方相同，有什麼地方不同？

三、　姜太公的才能在那一個地方？

四、　你知不知道有一個成語叫"姜太公釣魚"？

五、　三藏是誰？他對中國文化有何影響？

六、　和尚是什麼人？

七、　關於三藏取經的故事有一本小說，你知道嗎？

八、　你知道影響中國幾千年文化的思想有那些？

生字

1	姜	jiāng ㄐㄧㄤ	*a surname*
2	太公	tàigōng ㄊㄞˋ ㄍㄨㄥ	*Jiang's given name*
3	牛肉	niúròu ㄋㄧㄡˊ ㄖㄡˋ	*beef*
4	釣魚	diàoyú ㄉㄧㄠˋ ㄩˊ	*to go fishing*
5	魚鉤	yúgōu ㄩˊ ㄍㄡ	*fish hook*
6	魚餌	yúěr ㄩˊ ㄦˇ	*bait*
7	水面	shuǐmiàn ㄕㄨㄟˇ ㄇㄧㄢˋ	*surface of the water*
8	尺	chǐ ㄔˇ	*unit of length (1/3 of a meter)*
9	三藏	sānzhàng ㄙㄢ ㄓㄤˋ	*name of a monk*
10	取	qǔ ㄑㄩˇ	*to fetch*
11	經	jīng ㄐㄧㄥ	*scriptures*
12	唐朝	tángcháo ㄊㄤˊ ㄔㄠˊ	*the Tang Dynasty*
13	和尚	héshàng ㄏㄜˊ ㄕㄤˋ	*monk*
14	印度	yìndù ㄧㄣˋ ㄉㄨˋ	*India*
15	佛經	fójīng ㄈㄛˊ ㄐㄧㄥ	*Buddhist scriptures*
16	佛教	fójiào ㄈㄛˊ ㄐㄧㄠˋ	*Buddhism*
17	翻譯	fānyì ㄈㄢ ㄧˋ	*to translate*
18	出家	chūjiā ㄔㄨ ㄐㄧㄚ	*to leave the worldly life and become a monk*
19	道理	dàolǐ ㄉㄠˋ ㄌㄧˇ	*truth; reason*
20	決心	juéxīn ㄐㄩㄝˊ ㄒㄧㄣ	*determination*
21	沙漠	shāmò ㄕㄚ ㄇㄛˋ	*desert*
22	小說	xiǎoshuō ㄒㄧㄠˇ ㄕㄨㄛ	*a novel*

第十三章　太公钓鱼和三藏取经

大约在三千多年前，有一个很有才能的人。他曾帮助一个国王建立了一个持续八百年的朝代。这个人姓姜[1]，名字叫太公[2]。别人都叫他姜太公。姜太公虽然很有才能，可是他一生的机会都不好。一直到晚年的时候，他的生活才有了很大的变化。

传说，姜太公到了五十岁，还没有做成什麽事。他太太就离开他了。到了六十岁，他还在给别人卖牛肉[3]。七十岁的时候，他又卖起饭来。他的生活非常不好，就是自己一个人的吃和住，都成了问题。可是，姜太公一点也不会不高兴。他不觉得自己是一个无用的人，反而告诉别人，自己是一个很有用的人。

最後，姜太公来到一个小河边，开始钓起鱼来。人们不知道他是不是真的要钓鱼[4]，因为他钓鱼的方法非常特别。他用的鱼钩[5]是直的，也不用鱼饵[6]。而且，他的鱼钩是离开水面[7]三尺[8]以上，而不是在水中。所有的人看了，都说这种方法是不可能钓到鱼的。

但是，姜太公告诉人们，他真正要钓的不是鱼，而是一个机会。他要钓的是一个国王，他的意思是说，将有一个国王会来找他，请他为国王服务。这是他一生的机会。这个机会可以让他把他一生的才能都用出来。

这个机会终於来了。有一天，一个国王和他手下的人经过这个河边，发现了姜太公。国王非常喜欢太公的才能，可以帮助国王打仗，太公就成了皇宫里最重要的人之一。太公帮助国王打了很多仗，最後打败了另外一个大的国家。

三藏[9]取[10]经[11]

三藏是唐朝[12]时候的一位和尚[13]。他在中国历史上是非常有名的，因为他离开中国十七年，一个人去印度[14]学习佛经[15]，然後把佛教[16]带回到中国。他带回来的佛经有一千三百三十五本，并且把它们都翻译[17]成了中文。

三藏从小就出家[18]做了和尚。他非常喜欢读佛经，才二十多岁，就把他能找到的佛经都读完了。可是，他发现在中国，佛经很不完全。而且，三藏有很多的问题，也没有人能给他满意的回答。所以，三藏就决定自己去西方印度，在那里学习佛经和佛教的道理[19]。

那时候，交通很不方便，路又远，什麼事情都可能发生。可是，三藏因为有很大的决心[20]，不怕所有可能发生的事情，他一个人离开了中国。那时，三藏才二十六岁。一路上，他经过了许多的高山和沙漠[21]。最後他来到了印度。在印度，三藏学习了五年的佛学道理和许多古代的学问，在印度他是一个很有名的和尚。

三藏的名字被很多的国家和国王知道了，他们都希望能和他见面。三藏这时开始旅行，他一共走了五十六个国家，见到了许多的国王。他曾在七、八千人和十八个国王的前面，向大家谈佛教的道理。从那以後，三藏的名字就被更多的人知道了。这时，中国的皇帝才知道有一位和尚在印度很出名。

三藏回来时，他已经四十三岁了。他得到了皇帝的帮助，把带回来的佛经都翻译成了中文。他又写了一些书，把他去印度，一路上所看见的事情都告诉了人们。这本书後来被写成了小说[22]。三藏的一生，使佛教对中国文化有了很大的影响。

阅读理解

一、 姜太公是谁？

二、 姜太公和愚公有什麼地方相同，有什麼地方不同？

三、 姜太公的才能在那一个地方？

四、 你知不知道有一个成语叫"姜太公钓鱼"？

五、 三藏是谁？他对中国文化有何影响？

六、 和尚是什麼人？

七、 关於三藏取经的故事有一本小说，你知道吗？

八、 你知道影响中国几千年文化的思想有那些？

生字

1	姜	jiāng	a surname
2	太公	tàigōng	Jiang's given name
3	牛肉	niúròu	beef
4	钓鱼	diàoyú	to go fishing
5	鱼钩	yúgōu	fish hook
6	鱼饵	yúěr	bait
7	水面	shuǐmiàn	surface of the water
8	尺	chǐ	unit of length（1/3 of a meter）
9	三藏	sānzhàng	name of a monk
10	取	qǔ	to fetch
11	经	jīng	scriptures
12	唐朝	tángcháo	the Tang Dynasty
13	和尚	héshàng	monk
14	印度	yìndù	India
15	佛经	fójīng	Buddhist scriptures
16	佛教	fójiào	Buddhism
17	翻译	fānyì	to translate
18	出家	chūjiā	to leave the worldly life and become a monk
19	道理	dàolǐ	truth; reason
20	决心	juéxīn	determination
21	沙漠	shāmò	desert
22	小说	xiǎoshuō	a novel

Chapter 13   Tai Gong Goes Fishing and San Zhang

Fetches the Scriptures

About three thousand years ago, there lived a man with many capabilities. He helped a king establish a dynasty which lasted 800 years. His family name was Jiang and his given name was Tai Gong. Others called him Jiang Tai Gong. Although Jiang Tai Gong was very talented, he never had any opportunities in life. In his later years, however, a great change came over his life.

It is said that up until the age of fifty, Jiang Tai Gong never accomplished anything, so his wife left him. When he was sixty, he was still selling beef to people. When he was seventy, he started selling meals. His life was hard, just getting food and lodging for himself was difficult. However, Jiang Tai Gong was not unhappy at all. He didn't think of himself as a useless person; in fact, he told people that he was very useful.

At one point, he arrived at a river bank and he started to fish. The people couldn't tell if he really intended to fish because his method of fishing was so unusual. He had a straight fishhook but no bait. What is more, instead of putting the fishhook in the water, he kept it three chi from the surface of the water. The spectators commented that he couldn't catch any fish that way.

But Jiang Tai Gong told them that he didn't actually want to catch a fish, he wanted to catch an opportunity. He wanted to catch a king, which really meant that he wanted a king to invite him to come and work for him. This was the opportunity of his lifetime, with it he would be able to put to use the talents of an entire life.

In the end, his opportunity came. One day a king and his men were passing by the river when they saw Jiang Tai Gong. The king admired Jiang Tai Gong's many capabilities and thought he could help him win his wars. Jiang Tai Gong became one of the king's most important men. Tai Gong helped the king fight many wars and, in the end, they even defeated another country.

San Zhang Fetches the Scriptures

San Zhang was a monk who lived during the Tang Dynasty. He is a very famous historical figure in China because he left China and lived by himself in India for seventeen years where he studied the Buddhist Scriptures, eventually bringing Buddhism back to China. He brought back 1,335 volumes of scriptures and then translated them into Chinese.

As a boy, San Zhang had left the worldly life to become a monk. He really enjoyed reading the Buddhist Scriptures and discovered at the age of twenty that he had read all the scriptures he could find. He also discovered that Chinese Buddhist Scriptures were lacking something, and that he still had many questions to which no one could give him any satisfactory answers. Therefore, San Zhang decided to travel west to India where he could study the Buddhist Scriptures and the philosophy of Buddhism.

In those days, traveling was very difficult. The trip to India was long and anything could happen along the way. But San Zhang was determined to go and therefore not afraid of anything that might happen. He set out by himself, leaving China behind. San Zhang was only twenty-six at the time. Along the way he went over many mountains and passed through many deserts until he finally arrived in India. He spent five years studying the principles of Buddhism and other ancient knowledge. He became a famous monk in India.

San Zhang's name became known in many countries, and many kings wanted to meet him. So San Zhang began to travel. He traveled to fifty-six countries and met with many kings. He stood in front of 7,000-8,000 people and eighteen kings and talked about the basic truths of Buddhism. After that, his name was known to even more people. Even the emperor of China finally heard about this monk who had become so famous in India.

When San Zhang returned he was forty-three-years-old. He obtained the emperor's support to translate into Chinese the scriptures he had brought back. He also wrote books in which he told people about everything he saw on his travels to India. These books were later turned into a novel. Through San Zhang's life, Chinese culture was greatly affected by Buddhism.

第十四章　東郭先生和世外桃源

東郭先生

　　從前，有一個讀書人叫東郭[1]先生。因為讀書讀得太多了，就變得糊塗[2]起來，又沒有很多的力氣。一天，他在路上遇見了一隻狼[3]。狼非常害怕[4]地跑來，對東郭先生說：“先生，求[5]你救[6]救我，因為有獵人[7]在追我。如果你救了我，我永遠不會忘記你的。”東郭先生聽了，不知道怎麼辦。可是，他看到狼這麼的害怕，就把身上帶著的一個大口袋[8]打開，把狼放在裏面。然後，東郭先生就把口袋綁[9]起來了。

這時，獵人追上來見狼不見了，就問東郭先生說：“你看見一隻狼沒有？”東郭先生就說：“沒有。這裏的路有很多條，也許狼往別的路上跑了。”獵人聽了這話，就離開了。東郭先生這時把狼從口袋裏放出來了。

狼出來以後，對東郭先生說：“謝謝你救了我，可是求你再救我一次。因爲我現在餓得要死，所以我想把你吃了。如果你這次救了我，我一定永遠不會忘記你的。”東郭先生聽了，又糊塗起來，可是又不知道怎麼辦。正在這時，有一位老農[10]走了過來。東郭先生就對狼說，讓我們先問問老農吧！

東郭先生就把事情告訴了老農，說：“我上次已經救了它，這次還應當被它吃嗎？”狼就對老農說：“他如果不讓我吃，怎麼能救我呢？他不救我，讀那麼多的書有什麼用呢？我不吃他，怎麼能永遠記住他呢？”老農聽了，就對狼說：“我糊塗了，請從頭[11]再來一次吧！讓我看看，東郭先生是怎樣把你放在口袋裏的。”

狼就同意了，再一次走進了口袋裏，說：“請你們不要再糊塗了。快一點，因爲我已經很餓了。”等狼走進了口袋，老農就快快的把口袋綁起來。他對東郭先生說：“你怎麼這麼糊塗？讀了這麼多的書，你都不知道現在是應該救狼還是救人嗎？"說完，就拿起棒子把狼打死了。

世外[12]桃源[13]

從前有一個打魚人，打了一天的魚，沒有什麼結果。心裏很難過，對自己說："這個世界真是有很大的問題。打了一天的魚，怎麼就只有這幾條小魚呢？這麼小的魚就是貓[14]都不會吃的。我聽說在西方很遠的地方，有一個世界，打魚非常的容易。在那裏，打魚不是爲了吃魚，而是爲了使打魚的人心裏高興..."

想到他聽說的那個世界，打魚人就很高興。他繼續想下去："聽說，那裏的魚知道自己不會被燒來吃，所以都出來隨便讓人打。魚都知道，被打上去了，還是會被放回來的。"打魚人就想，要是我能去這樣一個地方真好，可以打到很多魚...想著想著，也不知過了多少時候，他突然發現自己來到了一個從來沒有看見過的地方。

這個地方非常特別，到處都是美麗的桃花[15]。這裏好像是一個天外[16]的世界。打魚人一進到這個地方，心裏覺得特別的高興。這時，有一個農人[17]走過來歡迎他，問他說："你是誰？你怎麼會到這裏來的？"打魚人回答說："我也不知道怎麼到這裏來的。你們這是什麼地方？怎麼會這麼的美？"

　　原來，農人告訴打魚人，這裏叫桃花源。世界上的人都不知道有這樣一個地方，這裏的人也不知道外面發生的事。這裏的生活很安靜，人人都有飯吃，人人也很喜歡工作。

　　打魚人來到桃花源的事情，很快地就讓這裏的人都知道了。大家都非常的高興，都請他去自己的家裏去作客[18]。打魚人就在桃花源住了幾天，他把自己的事告訴了這裏的人，大家才知道在外面的世界生活很不容易。他們說，如果不是因爲他是打魚人，他們就會留他永遠住在桃花源。可是，桃花源裏沒有魚打。

　　打魚人說，如果這裏的人一定要留他住下來，他會很高興的。他說，自己並不喜歡打魚，可是沒有魚吃，將是一件很難過的事情。除非這裏的人讓他常常出去，打一些魚回到這裏來吃。大家都說這樣不行，因爲你只能住在一個世界裏，住在兩個世界的人是不會幸福的。

　　打魚人說，不要緊[19]，他還是應該回去，因爲他還有家人和朋友在外面的世界裏，家人和朋友對他的生活也是非常重要的。他還告訴桃花源裏的人，聽說西方也有一個世界。在那裏也差不多像桃花源，那裏還可以打魚吃。不過，打魚人說，去西方的桃花源可能不像來這個桃花源容易。這個桃花源不太難找，可是聽說西方的那個桃花源，還要辦護照[20]簽證[21]。大家聽說了這些事，才知道外面的世界變化這麼大。

幾天後，打魚人就和桃花源裏的人說再見了。他出了桃花源以後，回到了家裏，就把發生的事和自己所見到的，都告訴了家裏的人和朋友。大家問他，這麼好的地方，你爲什麼要回來呢？打魚人說，他想回來帶大家一起去。他們就一起再去找桃花源，可是桃花源再也找不到了。

從那以後，打魚人的生活變得非常不幸福，因爲他還是不喜歡打魚，也不喜歡這個世界。可是，他既找不到桃花源，又[22]常常想著有一天能去西方的那個世界打魚。他這時才想起了桃花源裏的人告訴他的話：一個人只能活在一個世界上，不然生活是會非常沒有意思的。最後，打魚人死的時候，還是非常不幸福。因爲他一直還在想著西方的那個世界。

閱讀理解：

一、　東郭先生爲什麼糊塗？

二、　"難得糊塗"是什麼意思？談談你的看法。

三、　世上真的有世外桃源嗎？

四、　你希望真的有這麼一個地方嗎？

五、　如果當時是你發現了世外桃源，而你也知道只要一離開就再也找不這個地方，你會離開那裏嗎？

六、　有什麼地方是你心目中的世外桃源？

生字

[1] 東郭	dōngguō	ㄉㄨㄥ ㄍㄨㄛ	name of a well-read scholar
[2] 糊塗	hútú	ㄏㄨˊ ㄊㄨˊ	muddled; confused
[3] 狼	láng	ㄌㄤˊ	wolf
[4] 害怕	hàipà	ㄏㄞˋ ㄆㄚˋ	to fear
[5] 求	qiú	ㄑㄧㄡˊ	to save
[6] 救	jiù	ㄐㄧㄡˋ	to beg
[7] 獵人	lièrén	ㄌㄧㄝˋ ㄖㄣˊ	a hunter
[8] 口袋	kǒudài	ㄎㄡˇ ㄉㄞˋ	sack
[9] 綁	bǎng	ㄅㄤˇ	to tie up
[10] 老農	lǎonóng	ㄌㄠˇ ㄋㄨㄥˊ	old peasant
[11] 從頭	cóngtóu	ㄘㄨㄥˊ ㄊㄡˊ	from the beginning
[12] 世外	shìwài	ㄕˋ ㄨㄞˋ	away from our world
[13] 桃源	táoyuán	ㄊㄠˊ ㄩㄢˊ	a fictitious Land of Peach Blossoms; a place away from the turmoil of our world
[14] 貓	māo	ㄇㄠ	cat
[15] 桃花	táohuā	ㄊㄠˊ ㄏㄨㄚ	peach blossoms
[16] 天外	tiānwài	ㄊㄧㄢ ㄨㄞˋ	in another world
[17] 農人	nóngrén	ㄋㄨㄥˊ ㄖㄣˊ	peasant
[18] 作客	zuòkè	ㄗㄨㄛˋ ㄎㄜˋ	to be a guest
[19] 不要緊	búyàojǐn	ㄅㄨˊ ㄧㄠˋ ㄐㄧㄣˇ	do not worry
[20] 護照	hùzhào	ㄏㄨˋ ㄓㄠˋ	passport
[21] 簽證	qiānzhèng	ㄑㄧㄢ ㄓㄥˋ	visa
[22] 既…又…	jì…yòu…	ㄐㄧˋ…ㄧㄡˋ…	not only...but also…

第十四章　东郭先生和世外桃源

　　从前，有一个读书人叫东郭[1]先生。因为读书读得太多了，就变得糊涂[2]起来，又没有很多的力气。一天，他在路上遇见了一只狼[3]。狼非常害怕[4]地跑来，对东郭先生说："先生，求[5]你救[6]救我，因为有猎人[7]在追我。如果你救了我，我永远不会忘记你的。"东郭先生听了，不知道怎麽办。可是，他看到狼这麽的害怕，就把身上带著的一个大口袋[8]打开，把狼放在里面。然後，东郭先生就把口袋绑[9]起来了。

　　这时，猎人追上来见狼不见了，就问东郭先生说："你看见一只狼没有？"东郭先生就说："没有。这里的路有很多条，也许狼往别的路上跑了。"猎人听了这话，就离开了。东郭先生这时把狼从口袋里放出来了。

　　狼出来以後，对东郭先生说："谢谢你救了我，可是求你再救我一次。因为我现在饿得要死，所以我想把你吃了。如果你这次救了我，我一定永远不会忘记你的。"东郭先生听了，又糊涂起来，可是又不知道怎麽办。正在这时，有一位老农[10]走了过来。东郭先生就对狼说，让我们先问问老农吧！

东郭先生就把事情告诉了老农，说："我上次已经救了它，这次还应当被它吃吗？"狼就对老农说："他如果不让我吃，怎麼能救我呢？他不救我，读那麼多的书有什麼用呢？我不吃他，怎麼能永远记住他呢？"老农听了，就对狼说："我糊涂了，请从头[11]再来一次吧！让我看看，东郭先生是怎样把你放在口袋里的。"

狼就同意了，再一次走进了口袋里，说："请你们不要再糊涂了。快一点，因为我已经很饿了。"等狼走进了口袋，老农就快快的把口袋绑起来。他对东郭先生说："你怎麼这麼糊涂？读了这麼多的书，你都不知道现在是应该救狼还是救人吗？"说完，就拿起棒子把狼打死了。

世外[12]桃源[13]

从前有一个打鱼人，打了一天的鱼，没有什麼结果。心里很难过，对自己说："这个世界真是有很大的问题。打了一天的鱼，怎麼就只有这几条小鱼呢？这麼小的鱼就是猫[14]都不会吃的。我听说在西方很远的地方，有一个世界，打鱼非常的容易。在那里，打鱼不是为了吃鱼，而是为了使打鱼的人心里高兴…"

想到他听说的那个世界，打鱼人就很高兴。他继续想下去："听说，那里的鱼知道自己不会被烧来吃，所以都出来随便让人打。鱼都知道，被打上去了，还是会被放回来的。"打鱼人就想，要是我能去这样一个地方真好，可以打到很多鱼…想著想著，也不知过了多少时候，他突然发现自己来到了一个从来没有看见过的地方。

这个地方非常特别，到处都是美丽的桃花[15]。这里好像是一个天外[16]的世界。打鱼人一进到这个地方，心里觉得特别的高兴。这时，有一个农人[17]走过来欢迎他，问他说："你是谁？你怎麽会到这里来的？"打鱼人回答说："我也不知道怎麽到这里来的。你们这是什麽地方？怎麽会这麽的美？"

原来，农人告诉打鱼人，这里叫桃花源。世界上的人都不知道有这样一个地方，这里的人也不知道外面发生的事。这里的生活很安静，人人都有饭吃，人人也很喜欢工作。

打鱼人来到桃花源的事情，很快地就让这里的人都知道了。大家都非常的高兴，都请他去自己的家里去作客[18]。打鱼人就在桃花源住了几天，他把自己的事告诉了这里的人，大家才知道在外面的世界生活很不容易。他们说，如果不是因为他是打鱼人，他们就会留他永远住在桃花源。可是，桃花源里没有鱼打。

　　打鱼人说，如果这里的人一定要留他住下来，他会很高兴的。他说，自己并不喜欢打鱼，可是没有鱼吃，将是一件很难过的事情。除非这里的人让他常常出去，打一些鱼回到这里来吃。大家都说这样不行，因为你只能住在一个世界里，住在两个世界的人是不会幸福的。

　　打鱼人说，不要紧[19]，他还是应该回去，因为他还有家人和朋友在外面的世界里，家人和朋友对他的生活也是非常重要的。他还告诉桃花源里的人，听说西方也有一个世界。在那里也差不多像桃花源，那里还可以打鱼吃。不过，打鱼人说，去西方的桃花源可能不像来这个桃花源容易。这个桃花源不太难找，可是听说西方的那个桃花源，还要办护照[20]签证[21]。大家听说了这些事，才知道外面的世界变化这麽大。

　　几天後，打鱼人就和桃花源里的人说再见了。他出了桃花源以後，回到了家里，就把发生的事和自己所见到的，都告诉了家里的人和朋友。大家问他，这麽好的地方，你为什麽要回来呢？打鱼人说，他想回来带大家一起去。他们就一起再去找桃花源，可是桃花源再也找不到了。

　　从那以後，打鱼人的生活变得非常不幸福，因为他还是不喜欢打鱼，也不喜欢这个世界。可是，他既找不到桃花源，又[22]常常想著有一天能去西方的那个世界打鱼。他这时才想起了桃花源里的人告诉他的话：一个人只能活在一个世界上，不然生活是会非常没有意思的。最後，打鱼人死的时候，还是非常不幸福。因为他一直还在想著西方的那个世界。

阅读理解：

一、　东郭先生为什麼糊涂？

二、　"难得糊涂"是什麼意思？谈谈你的看法。

三、　世上真的有世外桃源吗？

四、　你希望真的有这麼一个地方吗？

五、　如果当时是你发现了世外桃源，而你也知道只要一离开就再也找不这个地方，你会离开那里吗？

六、　有什麼地方是你心目中的世外桃源？

生字

1	东郭	dōngguō	name of a well-read scholar
2	糊涂	hútú	muddled; confused
3	狼	láng	wolf
4	害怕	hàipà	to fear
5	求	qiú	to save
6	救	jiù	to beg
7	猎人	lièrén	a hunter
8	口袋	kǒudài	sack
9	绑	bǎng	to tie up
10	老农	lǎonóng	old peasant
11	从头	cóngtóu	from the beginning
12	世外	shìwài	away from our world
13	桃源	táoyuán	a fictitious Land of Peach Blossoms; a place away from the turmoil of our world
14	猫	māo	cat
15	桃花	táohuā	peach blossoms
16	天外	tiānwài	in another world
17	农人	nóngrén	peasant
18	作客	zuòkè	to be a guest
19	不要紧	búyàojǐn	do not worry
20	护照	hùzhào	passport
21	签证	qiānzhèng	visa
22	既⋯又⋯	jì⋯yòu⋯	not only ⋯but also⋯

Chapter 14　Mr. Dong Guo and the Land of Peach Blossoms

There once was a scholar named Mr. Dong Guo. Because he read too many books, he became quite muddled in his head. He was also a man of little physical strength. One day he bumped into a wolf along the road. The wolf was running towards him looking terrified and he said to Mr. Dong Guo, "Please, sir, save me! There is a hunter chasing me. If you rescue me I'll remember you forever." When Mr. Dong Guo heard this, he didn't know what to do. But because the wolf looked so scared, he opened the large sack that he had been carrying and put the wolf inside. Then Mr. Dong Guo tied up the sack.

Soon the hunter arrived and when he didn't see the wolf anywhere, he asked Mr. Dong Guo, "Have you seen a wolf around?" Mr. Dong Guo said, "No. This road has many branches, maybe he ran off along another road." When the hunter heard this, he left and Mr. Dong Guo released the wolf from the sack.

As soon as the wolf was out, he said to Mr. Dong Guo, "Thank you for saving my life, but please, save me one more time. I am starving to death and I want to eat you. If you save me just one more time, I will definitely never forget you." When Mr. Dong Guo heard this, he was very confused again and didn't know what to do. Just then an old peasant walked by and Mr. Dong Guo said to the wolf, "Let us ask the old peasant what to do."

So Mr. Dong Guo explained the situation and asked the old peasant, "I saved his life the last time, do I have to let him eat me now?" Then the wolf said to the old peasant, "If he doesn't let me eat him, how can he be saving me? If he doesn't save me, what is the use of reading all those books? If I don't eat him, how will I remember him forever?" The old peasant listened and then said to the wolf, "I'm confused, please explain the whole thing from the beginning. Could you show me how Mr. Dong Guo put you into the sack?"

The wolf agreed to get back into the sack. He said, "This time, please don't get confused again and hurry up because I am already very hungry." The old peasant waited until the wolf was back in the sack and then he quickly tied it up. He said to Mr. Dong Guo, "How can you be so muddle-headed? You have read so many books and you still don't know who to save, the wolf or the man?" Then the old peasant picked up an object and beat the wolf to death.

The Land of Peach Blossoms

There once was a fisherman who fished all day long with no success. He was very sad and said to himself, "This world is full of problems. You spend a whole day fishing and all you catch are a few tiny fish. These fish are so small that even a cat wouldn't eat them. I've heard of a world far away in the west where it is easy to catch fish. Fishermen there don't go fishing for food, they do it for their own pleasure."

Thinking about the land that he had heard of made the fisherman very happy. He continued thinking: I've heard that the fish in that place know that they won't be cooked and eaten, so they easily let themselves be caught. The fish know that if they are caught, they will be released again. The fisherman thought how wonderful it would be to go to such a place and catch many fish, and as he was imagining this, no one knows how much time passed, but he suddenly found himself in a place he had never seen before.

It was an extraordinary place with peach blossoms blooming everywhere. It seemed like a land outside of his world. As soon as the fisherman stepped into this land, he felt extremely happy. A peasant came towards him to welcome him and asked, "Who are you? How is it that you came here?" The fisherman answered, "I don't know how I came here either. What is this place? How come it is so beautiful?"

The peasant told the fisherman that it was called the Land of Peach Blossoms. The fisherman had never heard of such a place, and he knew that the rest of the people on earth hadn't heard of such a place either. He then discovered that the people in the Land of Peach Blossoms knew nothing of the world outside theirs. "Life here is very peaceful," they said. "The people have enough to eat and they enjoy working."

Soon all the people in the Land of Peach Blossoms knew about the fisherman's arrival. They were pleased and wanted to invite him into their homes to be their guest. The fisherman spent several days in this Land of Peach Blossoms. He told the people about his life and the people finally understood that life in his world was not easy. They said that if he were not a fisherman, they would ask him to stay with them forever, but unfortunately, there were no fish in the Land of Peach Blossoms.

The fisherman said that he would be very happy to stay in the Land of Peach Blossoms if the people here wanted him to. He didn't like fishing all that much, but not being able to eat fish would indeed be very sad. If only the people here would allow him to leave every now and then so that he could go catch some fish and bring them back to eat. They all said that that would not be possible because one could only live in one world. The people who lived in two worlds could never be happy.

The fisherman told them not to worry, but that he did have to return home because he had a family and friends living on the outside, and his family and friends were very important to him. He also told the people of the Land of Peach Blossoms that he had heard of another place in the west that was similar to the Land of Peach Blossoms, except that in the western Land of Peach Blossoms, one could also catch fish for food. The fisherman also said that going to the western Land of Peach Blossoms would not be as easy as coming to this Land of Peach Blossoms. This one was not difficult to find, but he had heard that a passport and visa were needed to go to the western one. When the people heard this, they realized how different the outside world was from theirs.

A few days later, the fisherman bid farewell to the people of the Land of Peach Blossoms. After he left the Land of Peach Blossoms, he returned home and told his family and friends all about what had happened and what he had seen. They asked him, if the place was so beautiful, why did he decide to come back? The fisherman answered that he had come home so that he could take everyone back with him. So they all set out to look for the Land of Peach Blossoms. However, they never found it again.

From then on, the fisherman's life was very unhappy. He still didn't enjoy fishing and he didn't like his world. Now that he couldn't find the Land of Peach Blossoms, he often dreamed about going fishing in that western world. He suddenly remembered what the people in the Land of Peach Blossoms had told him: A person can only live in one world, otherwise his life will become unbearable. In the end, at the time of his death, the fisherman was still unhappy because all he could think about was going to that western world.

第十五章　孔明借箭和花果猴王

孔明借箭

　　三國的時候，有一次，曹操帶著大軍[1]要和東吳[2]國打仗。兩個國家的大軍就準備在長江上打仗。因爲在水上打仗，箭是最重要的。東吳國希望能有很多的箭，東吳國就請一位叫孔明[3]的人來幫助，希望他能在十天內[4]，做成十萬隻箭。

　　孔明是當時一位非常有名的人。他很有天才，特別聰明，很懂[5]得怎麼打仗。他其實並不是東吳國的人，他是在另一個國家爲國王服務的，是東吳國請他來幫助的。孔明就說：“沒問題。十萬隻箭只要三天就可以了。”

　　三天的時間很快就要過去了。孔明就讓人準備二十隻大船，每一隻船上都要準備一千個稻草人[6]。人們就準備了船和兩萬個稻草人。稻草人都是一個一個站著的，看起來就像一船一船的兵[7]，他們又在每隻船上準備了很多鼓和三十個打鼓[8]的兵。孔明還要人準備一點酒和菜。

　　第三天到了，孔明就叫人把船開到長江裏去，船向著曹操的大軍開過去。這時剛剛是早上二點鐘的時候，長江上什麼也看不見。船快到曹操大軍面前的時候，孔明就叫人把船停下來，排[9]成一排。他叫每隻船上的人用力打起鼓來，好像是要開始打仗一樣。

　　有人很怕曹操的大軍會打過來，孔明不但不怕，還和朋友一起喝起酒來。孔明說，天這麼黑，什麼也看不見，曹操怎麼會出來呢？他一定會叫人放箭，這樣，我們的稻草人就可以把箭都接住[10]。

　　因爲天很黑，打鼓的聲音[11]非常大，曹操以爲東吳國的大軍打過來了。他就叫他的十萬兵不停地放箭。

到了天亮的時候，曹操才知道不好了。長江上並沒有東吳國的大軍，只是一些裝滿了稻草人的船隻，那些稻草人身上都是滿滿的箭，這時孔明叫人把船開回去。他們回去把箭全部拿下來，數一數，一共得到了十萬隻。

花果猴王

在很遠的東方，有一座山叫花果山[12]。山上有一個很大的石頭，過了不知道多少年，有一天，這個石頭突然"轟"的一聲開了。從裏面跑出來了一隻猴子[13]，兩眼發光[14]。因為它是從石頭裏生出來的，所以人們就叫它石猴。石猴在花果山上找到了許多的猴子朋友，天天一起玩，一起吃水果，非常高興。慢慢的，石猴就成了猴子朋友們的王。從那以後，它的名字就叫花果山猴王。

有一天，猴王突然哭了起來。其他的小猴子們很怕，不知道是什麼事。猴王說，我們今天玩得很高興。可是，我們老了以後都會死去。那時候我們怎麼辦呢？它這一說，所有的小猴子都哭起來了。這時，一隻猴子說："王啊，您應該離開花果山，到外面去求神仙[15]，找一個長生不老[16]的方法。"猴王聽了很高興，決定到外面去走一走。他希望能找到一個不死的方法。

　　猴王做了一隻很簡單的木船，坐船到海裏去找神仙，以求得一條不死的路。它在海裏過了八、九年，來到了西方的一個地方。猴王就上了一座高山，最後找到了一位神仙。神仙問它說：“你叫什麼名字？”猴王回答說：“我從小沒有父母，所以沒有名字。我是從石頭裏生出來的。”

　　猴王就跟著這位神仙學功夫。每天早上也學，晚上也學。猴王學了六、七年，就不想學了。它對神仙說：“我離開家到這麼遠的地方來，不是要學一些功夫，而是要找到一個不死的方法。請師父教我吧！”神仙聽了，就把長生不老的方法教給了猴王。猴王得到了這個方法非常高興，它告訴神仙，它現在想回家了，它想回去做王，因為在外面永遠不能做王。它和神仙說了再見，就回到了花果山。後來猴王才發現，它得到的不死的方法，只能讓它活三百四十年。

閱讀理解：

一、 孔明是誰？

二、 談談你所知道孔明的故事。

三、 石猴是怎樣來的？

四、 石猴為什麼要去外面求仙？

五、 最後石猴有沒有找到長生不老的方法？

生字

1 大軍	dàjūn	ㄉㄚˋ ㄐㄩㄣ	*army*
2 東吳	dōngwú	ㄉㄨㄥ ㄨˊ	*Eastern Wu*
3 孔明	kǒngmíng	ㄎㄨㄥˇ ㄇㄧㄥˊ	*name of a man*
4 十天內	shítiānnèi	ㄕˊ ㄊㄧㄢ ㄋㄟˋ	*within ten days*
5 懂	dǒng	ㄉㄨㄥˇ	*to understand*
6 稻草人	dàocǎorén	ㄉㄠˋ ㄘㄠˇ ㄖㄣˊ	*straw scarecrows*
7 兵	bīng	ㄅㄧㄥ	*soldiers*
8 打鼓	dǎgǔ	ㄉㄚˇ ㄍㄨˇ	*to beat drums*
9 排	pái	ㄆㄞˊ	*line up; a row; a line*
10 接住	jiēzhù	ㄐㄧㄝ ㄓㄨˋ	*to get; to receive*
11 聲音	shēngyīn	ㄕㄥ ㄧㄣ	*voice*
12 花果山	huāguǒshān	ㄏㄨㄚ ㄍㄨㄛˇ ㄕㄢ	*Mount Hua Guo*
13 猴子	hóuzi	ㄏㄡˊ ㄗ·	*monkey*
14 發光	fāguāng	ㄈㄚ ㄍㄨㄤ	*to shine*
15 神仙	shénxiān	ㄕㄣˊ ㄒㄧㄢ	*supernatural being*
16 長生不老	chángshēngbùlǎo	ㄔㄤˊ ㄕㄥ ㄅㄨˋ ㄌㄠˇ	*perpetual rejuvenation*

第十五章　孔明借箭和花果猴王

三国的时候，有一次，曹操带著大军[1]要和东吴[2]国打仗。两个国家的大军就准备在长江上打仗。因为在水上打仗，箭是最重要的。东吴国希望能有很多的箭，东吴国就请一位叫孔明[3]的人来帮助，希望他能在十天内[4]，做成十万只箭。

孔明是当时一位非常有名的人。他很有天才，特别聪明，很懂[5]得怎麼打仗。他其实并不是东吴国的人，他是在另一个国家为国王服务的，是东吴国请他来帮助的。孔明就说："没问题。十万只箭只要三天就可以了。"

三天的时间很快就要过去了。孔明就让人准备二十只大船，每一只船上都要准备一千个稻草人[6]。人们就准备了船和两万个稻草人。稻草人都是一个一个站著的，看起来就像一船一船的兵[7]，他们又在每只船上准备了很多鼓和三十个打鼓[8]的兵。孔明还要人准备一点酒和菜。

第三天到了，孔明就叫人把船开到长江里去，船向著曹操的大军开过去。这时刚刚是早上二点钟的时候，长江上什麼也看不见。船快到曹操大军面前的时候，孔明就叫人把船停下来，排[9]成一排。他叫每只船上的人用力打起鼓来，好像是要开始打仗一样。

有人很怕曹操的大军会打过来，孔明不但不怕，还和朋友一起喝起酒来。孔明说，天这麼黑，什麼也看不见，曹操怎麼会出来呢？他一定会叫人放箭，这样，我们的稻草人就可以把箭都接住[10]。

因为天很黑，打鼓的声音[11]非常大，曹操以为东吴国的大军打过来了。他就叫他的十万兵不停地放箭。到了天亮的时候，曹操才知道不好了。长江上并没有东吴国的大军，只是一些装满了稻草人的船只，那些稻草人身上都是满满的箭，这时孔明叫人把船开回去。他们回去把箭全部拿下来，数一数，一共得到了十万只。

花果猴王

在很远的东方，有一座山叫花果山[12]。山上有一个很大的石头，过了不知道多少年，有一天，这个石头突然"轰"的一声开了。从里面跑出来了一只猴子[13]，两眼发光[14]。因为它是从石头里生出来的，所以人们就叫它石猴。石猴在花果山上找到了许多的猴子朋友，天天一起玩，一起吃水果，非常高兴。慢慢的，石猴就成了猴子朋友们的王。从那以後，它的名字就叫花果山猴王。

有一天，猴王突然哭了起来。其他的小猴子们很怕，不知道是什麽事。猴王说，我们今天玩得很高兴。可是，我们老了以後都会死去。那时候我们怎麽办呢？它这一说，所有的小猴子都哭起来了。这时，一只猴子说："王啊，您应该离开花果山，到外面去求神仙[15]，找一个长生不老[16]的方法。"猴王听了很高兴，决定到外面去走一走。他希望能找到一个不死的方法。

猴王做了一只很简单的木船，坐船到海里去找神仙，以求得一条不死的路。它在海里过了八、九年，来到了西方的一个地方。猴王就上了一座高山，最後找到了一位神仙。神仙问它说："你叫什麽名字？"猴王回答说："我从小没有父母，所以没有名字。我是从石头里生出来的。"

猴王就跟著这位神仙学功夫。每天早上也学，晚上也学。猴王学了六、七年，就不想学了。它对神仙说："我离开家到这麽远的地方来，不是要学一些功夫，而是要找到一个不死的方法。请师父教我吧！"神仙听了，就把长生不老的方法教给了猴王。猴王得到了这个方法非常高兴，它告诉神仙，它现在想回家了，它想回去做王，因为在外面永远不能做王。它和神仙说了再见，就回到了花果山。後来猴王才发现，它得到的不死的方法，只能让它活三百四十年。

阅读理解：

一、　孔明是谁？

二、　谈谈你所知道孔明的故事。

三、　石猴是怎样来的？

四、　石猴为什麽要去外面求仙？

五、　最後石猴有没有找到长生不老的方法？

生字

1	大军	dàjūn	army
2	东吴	dōngwú	Eastern Wu
3	孔明	kǒngmíng	name of a man
4	十天内	shítiānnèi	within ten days
5	懂	dǒng	to understand
6	稻草人	dàocǎorén	straw scarecrows
7	兵	bīng	soldiers
8	打鼓	dǎgǔ	to beat drums
9	排	pái	line up; a row; a line
10	接住	jiēzhù	to get; to receive
11	声音	shēngyīn	voice
12	花果山	huāguǒshān	Mount Hua Guo
13	猴子	hóuzi	monkey
14	发光	fāguāng	to shine
15	神仙	shénxiān	supernatural being
16	长生不老	chángshēngbùlǎo	perpetual rejuvenation

Chapter 15   Kung Ming Borrows Arrows and the Monkey King of Mount Hua Guo

Once upon a time during the Three Kingdoms, Cao Cao lead his army to fight against the Kingdom of Wu. The two armies prepared to fight on the Yangtze River. When a battle took place on the water, it was best to use arrows, and the Kingdom of Wu wanted to have plenty of arrows. A man named Kung Ming was asked to help them in the hope that he would be able to make 100,000 arrows within ten days.

Kung Ming was a very famous man of the time. He was very talented, very intelligent, and extremely knowledgeable in the art of war. Although Kung Ming was not from the Kingdom of Wu, he actually served another king in another country, he willingly agreed to help the Kingdom of Wu. "No problem," he said, "I can make 100,000 arrows in three days."

When the three days were almost over, Kung Ming ordered twenty ships to be prepared. He told his men to prepare 1,000 straw scarecrows to put onto each ship. The men got the ships and prepared 20,000 scarecrows. The scarecrows were placed standing up on the ships to make it look like an army on a fleet of ships. They also placed many drums on the ships and thirty soldiers to drum the huge drums. Kung Ming then asked them to prepare some wine and food.

On the third day, Kung Ming ordered his men to sail the ships to the Yangtze River. They headed towards the opposite bank where Cao Cao's army was stationed. It was exactly two o'clock in the morning and there was no visibility at all. When the boats were about to arrive in front of Cao Cao's army, Kung Ming ordered the ships to stop and to line up in a row. Then he ordered the men on the ships to beat the drums with all their might. It sounded as if the war had begun.

Some people had been afraid that Cao Cao's army would rush over and battle with them, but not Kung Ming. Not only was he not afraid, but he sat down with his friends and started drinking wine. Kung Ming said, "When it is so dark that you can't see a thing, how could Cao Cao come over here? He will surely order his men to shoot their arrows, and that way, our scarecrows will receive all of their arrows."

Because of the darkness and the loud drumming, Cao Cao imagined that the army of the Kingdom of Wu had started its attack. He ordered his 100,000 soldiers to shoot arrows without stopping. When dawn arrived, he saw his mistake. There was no army of the Eastern Kingdom of Wu on the Yangtze at all, there were just a few ships filled with scarecrows. The bodies of the scarecrows were entirely loaded with arrows. At that moment, Kung Ming ordered the ships to retreat. As they traveled back they took each arrow out one by one: altogether, there were 100,000 arrows.

The Monkey King of Mount Hua Guo

Far in the east is a mountain called Mount Hua Guo. There was a very large rock on top of the mountain. One day, no one knows exactly after how many years, the rock made a loud rumbling noise, and a monkey with shining eyes jumped out of the rock. Because he had been born from a rock, the people called him Stone Monkey. The Stone Monkey made friends with lots of other monkeys on Mount Hua Guo. They played together, ate fruit together, and were very happy. Slowly but surely, the Stone Monkey turned into the king of the monkeys, and he was known as the Monkey King of Mount Hua Guo.

One day the Monkey King burst into tears. The other little monkeys were very worried, they didn't know what was wrong. The Monkey King said, "Today we had a lot of fun playing, however, when we get old, we will all die. Then what are we going to do?" When the other monkeys heard this, they all started to cry. Then one little monkey said, "My King, you must leave Mount Hua Guo to ask the supernatural beings for a method of perpetual rejuvenation." The Monkey King was encouraged to hear this and decided to set out. He hoped to find a way to avoid dying.

The Monkey King built a very simple wooden boat and sailed down a river to the sea in search of the supernatural beings to ask them about a path to immortality. After spending eight or nine years on the sea, he arrived at a place located in the west. The Monkey King climbed a tall mountain where he finally met a supernatural being. The being asked him, "What is your name?" The Monkey King answered, "I never had any parents, so I don't have a name. I was born from a rock."

The Monkey King began to follow the supernatural being and from him, learned Kung Fu. He practiced every morning and he practiced every evening. The Monkey King studied for six or seven years until he didn't feel like studying any more. He said to the supernatural being, "I didn't come all this way to simply study Kung Fu, what I really want is to become immortal. Please, master, teach me that!" When the supernatural being heard this, he taught the Monkey King the way to immortality. When the Monkey King had received this knowledge, he felt extremely happy. He told the supernatural being that he now intended to go home and be king because outside of his home he could never be king. He said good-bye to the supernatural being and returned to Mount Hua Guo. It was not until later that the Monkey King discovered that what he had learned about immortality was only enough to live for 340 years.

第十六章　成語故事

守株待兔

自相矛盾

守¹株²待³兔

　　有一個農夫很不喜歡種田，但是沒有辦法，每天他還是需要去田裏工作。在田裏的時候，農夫就常常在想，有沒有別的辦法可以有飯吃，又不用出來種地呢？他正想到這裏，突然看見一隻兔子[4]從田裏跑出來，不小心撞[5]到了一棵樹，兔子就死去了。

農夫高興地跑到樹下，拿起了兔子，自己對自己說："這不是一個很好的辦法嗎？今天沒有種地，就有飯吃了。我為什麼不每天這樣做呢？"想到這裏，農夫就決定再也不種地了。從那天以後，農夫就每天坐在樹底下等，希望有兔子會從田裏跑出來，撞到這棵樹上來。可是，農夫等了很久，並沒有看見一個兔子跑出來。他是不是已經餓昏[6]了呢。

自相矛盾[7]

古時候，有一個人在街上賣矛[8]和盾[9]。他對人說："我的矛是世界上最好的矛，什麼東西都可以刺[10]破。"然後，他拿起矛來刺很多的東西，沒有一樣不被刺破的。很多人聽了他的話，又看見他刺破的東西，就覺得他的矛真是非常好，人們就相信他說的話。

這時，他又拿起他要賣的盾來，對大家說："我的盾是世界上最好的盾，什麼東西都不能刺破它。"然後，他就拿起盾來，用很多的東西來刺它。真的，沒有一樣東西可以刺破這個盾。大家就又相信他的話了，覺得他的盾也是非常的好。

這時，有一個人開口了。他問賣矛和盾的人說："用你自己的矛，來刺你自己的盾，結果會怎樣呢？"賣矛和盾的人，什麼話也說不出來了。

刻舟[11]求劍[12]

有一個楚國[13]人坐了一隻小船過河。剛開船的時候，一不小心，他身上的劍掉[14]到河裏去了。當時，這個楚國人因為有急事[15]要過河去辦，所以就沒有馬上到水裏去找。為了記住劍掉下去的地方，楚國人就在船的邊上刻了一個記號[16]，說劍是從這個地方掉到水裏去的。然後，楚國人就過河辦事[17]去了。辦事回來，楚國人就在刻了記號的地方下水去找。可是，他找來找去怎麼也找不到了。

孟母[18]三遷[19]

中國古時候有一個大思想家，他的名字叫孟子[20]。孟子是是孔子的學生。孟子的母親很注意教小孩子，她希望能使小孩子在小的時候就能學好。孟子的母親也特別注意，小孩子的生活環境[21]是不是很好，因為環境對小孩子的影響也是很大的。

傳說，孟子小的時候，很會學別人的樣子，而且一學就會。有一天，孟子的母親看見孟子學別人死了以後，親人在哭的樣子。他的母親覺得，他們家住在墳墓的附近對孩子不好。孟子天天所看見的都是人死了，所以他學的也是關於人死了以後的事情。所以，她就決定搬家，離開原來住的地方。

　　他們搬了一個新的地方，這次搬到一個菜市場[22]附近，孟子的母親發現，孟子每天都在學別人做生意，孟子的母親覺得這個地方也不好。所以，他們就再次離開住的地方，搬到別的地方去了。

　　這一次，他們搬到了學校的附近。孟子就開始學人讀書的樣子。他開始讀書、寫字、人變得安靜起來。這次，孟子的母親就很喜歡這個地方。後來孟子長大了，很有學問，成了很有名的人。

閱讀理解：

一、　什麼是成語？

二、　你還知道其它的成語故事嗎？

三、　世界上有沒有守株待兔的人？

四、　說一個你所知道的自相矛盾的事。

五、　孟子的母親為什麼要三次搬家？

六、　你常常搬家嗎？為了什麼原因搬家？

七、　請你用這四個成語各造一個句子。

刻舟求劍

生字

¹ 守	shǒu	ㄕㄡˇ	to keep watch
² 株	zhū	ㄓㄨ	trunk of a tree
³ 待	dài	ㄉㄞˋ	to wait
⁴ 兔子	tùzi	ㄊㄨˋ ㄗ·	hare
⁵ 撞	zhuàng	ㄓㄨㄤˋ	to bump against
⁶ 昏	hūn	ㄏㄨㄣ	dizzy
⁷ 自相矛盾	zìxiāngmáodùn	ㄗˋ ㄒㄧㄤ ㄇㄠˊ ㄉㄨㄣˋ	self-contradiction
⁸ 矛	máo	ㄇㄠˊ	spear
⁹ 盾	dùn	ㄉㄨㄣˋ	shield
¹⁰ 刺	cì	ㄘˋ	to pierce
¹¹ 刻舟	kèzhōu	ㄎㄜˋ ㄓㄡ	to carve onto the boat
¹² 求劍	qiújiàn	ㄑㄧㄡˊ ㄐㄧㄢˋ	to seek for the sword
¹³ 楚國	chǔguó	ㄔㄨˇ ㄍㄨㄛˊ	the Kingdom of Chu
¹⁴ 掉	diào	ㄉㄧㄠˋ	to drop; to fall
¹⁵ 急事	jíshì	ㄐㄧˊ ㄕˋ	urgent business
¹⁶ 記號	jìhào	ㄐㄧˋ ㄏㄠˋ	a mark; a sign
¹⁷ 辦事	bànshì	ㄅㄢˋ ㄕˋ	to take care of affairs
¹⁸ 孟母	mèngmǔ	ㄇㄥˋ ㄇㄨˇ	Mencius' mother
¹⁹ 三遷	sānqiān	ㄙㄢ ㄑㄧㄢ	to move three times
²⁰ 孟子	mèngzǐ	ㄇㄥˋ ㄗˇ	Mencius
²¹ 環境	huánjìng	ㄏㄨㄢˊ ㄐㄧㄥˋ	environment
²² 菜市場	càishìcháng	ㄘㄞˋ ㄕˋ ㄔㄤˊ	vegetable market

第十六章　成语故事

守¹株²待³兔

　　有一个农夫很不喜欢种田，但是没有办法，每天他还是需要去田里工作。在田里的时候，农夫就常常在想，有没有别的办法可以有饭吃，又不用出来种地呢？他正想到这里，突然看见一只兔子⁴从田里跑出来，不小心撞⁵到了一棵树，兔子就死去了。

　　农夫高兴地跑到树下，拿起了兔子，自己对自己说："这不是一个很好的办法吗？今天没有种地，就有饭吃了。我为什麼不每天这样做呢？"想到这里，农夫就决定再也不种地了。从那天以後，农夫就每天坐在树底下等，希望有兔子会从田里跑出来，撞到这棵树上来。可是，农夫等了很久，并没有看见一个兔子跑出来。他是不是已经饿昏⁶了呢。

自相矛盾[7]

古时候，有一个人在街上卖矛[8]和盾[9]。他对人说："我的矛是世界上最好的矛，什麽东西都可以刺[10]破。"然後，他拿起矛来刺很多的东西，没有一样不被刺破的。很多人听了他的话，又看见他刺破的东西，就觉得他的矛真是非常好，人们就相信他说的话。

这时，他又拿起他要卖的盾来，对大家说："我的盾是世界上最好的盾，什麽东西都不能刺破它。"然後，他就拿起盾来，用很多的东西来刺它。真的，没有一样东西可以刺破这个盾。大家就又相信他的话了，觉得他的盾也是非常的好。

这时，有一个人开口了。他问卖矛和盾的人说："用你自己的矛，来刺你自己的盾，结果会怎样呢？"卖矛和盾的人，什麽话也说不出来了。

刻舟[11]求剑[12]

有一个楚国[13]人坐了一只小船过河。刚开船的时候，一不小心，他身上的剑掉[14]到河里去了。当时，这个楚国人因为有急事[15]要过河去办，所以就没有马上到水里去找。为了记住剑掉下去的地方，楚国人就在船的边上刻了一个记号[16]，说剑是从这个地方掉到水里去的。然後，楚国人就过河办事[17]去了。办事回来，楚国人就在刻了记号的地方下水去找。可是，他找来找去怎麼也找不到了。

孟母[18]三迁[19]

中国古时候有一个大思想家，他的名字叫孟子[20]。孟子是是孔子的学生。孟子的母亲很注意教小孩子，她希望能使小孩子在小的时候就能学好。孟子的母亲也特别注意，小孩子的生活环境[21]是不是很好，因为环境对小孩子的影响也是很大的。

传说，孟子小的时候，很会学别人的样子，而且一学就会。有一天，孟子的母亲看见孟子学别人死了以後，亲人在哭的样子。他的母亲觉得，他们家住在坟墓的附近对孩子不好。孟子天天所看见的都是人死了，所以他学的也是关於人死了以後的事情。所以，她就决定搬家，离开原来住的地方。

他们搬了一个新的地方，这次搬到一个菜市场[22]附近，孟子的母亲发现，孟子每天都在学别人做生意，孟子的母亲觉得这个地方也不好。所以，他们就再次离开住的地方，搬到别的地方去了。

这一次，他们搬到了学校的附近。孟子就开始学人读书的样子。他开始读书、写字、人变得安静起来。这次，孟子的母亲就很喜欢这个地方。後来孟子长大了，很有学问，成了很有名的人。

阅读理解：

一、　什麼是成语？

二、　你还知道其它的成语故事吗？

三、　世界上有没有守株待兔的人？

四、　说一个你所知道的自相矛盾的事。

五、　孟子的母亲为什麼要三次搬家？

六、　你常常搬家吗？为了什麼原因搬家？

七、　请你用这四个成语各造一个句子。

生字

1	守	shǒu	to keep watch
2	株	zhū	trunk of a tree
3	待	dài	to wait
4	兔子	tùzi	hare
5	撞	zhuàng	to bump against
6	昏	hūn	dizzy
7	自相矛盾	zìxiāngmáodùn	self-contradiction
8	矛	máo	spear
9	盾	dùn	shield
10	刺	cì	to pierce
11	刻舟	kèzhōu	to carve onto the boat
12	求剑	qiújiàn	to seek for the sword
13	楚国	chǔguó	the Kingdom of Chu
14	掉	diào	to drop; to fall
15	急事	jíshì	urgent business
16	记号	jìhào	a mark; a sign
17	办事	bànshì	to take care of affairs
18	孟母	mèngmǔ	Mencius' mother
19	三迁	sānqiān	to move three times
20	孟子	mèngzǐ	Mencius
21	环境	huánjìng	environment
22	菜市场	càishìcháng	vegetable market

Chapter 16   Idioms

Standing by a Tree Hoping to Catch a Hare

There once was a farmer who really didn't like farming. But there was nothing he could do about it, he had to go out everyday to work in the fields. While he was out there, he often wondered whether there was no other way to obtain food without cultivating the land. Just then he saw a hare running across the field. As it was not paying attention, it dashed into a tree, fell over, and died.

The farmer ran over to the tree and picked up the hare and happily said to himself, "This is a wonderful method! I didn't work in the fields today, and still I have food to eat. I should try this everyday." Right away the farmer decided that he would no longer work in the fields. From that day on, the farmer sat under the tree waiting and hoping that another hare would come running across the field and bump into the tree. However, he never did see another hare running in the field. Do you think he was dizzy from lack of food?

Self-Contradiction

In ancient times, there was a man who sold spears and shields on the street. He told people, "My spears are the best in the world, they can pierce absolutely anything." Then he demonstrated how the spears could pierce all kinds of things--nothing withheld the power of the spears. Many people heard what he said and went to watch as he pierced through things with his spears; they saw that his spears were truly very good and they believed him.

Then he took out a shield and said to the people, "My shields are the best shields in the whole world, nothing at all can pierce through them." He took out a shield and demonstrated with all kinds of things how strong his shield was. Truly, nothing was able to pierce through it. Again, the people believed him and felt that his shields were really the best.

Suddenly someone piped up and said to the salesman, "What will happen if you use your own spear to pierce your own shield?" The salesman had nothing more to say.

Carving a Mark on the Boat to Seek the Sword

A man from the Kingdom of Chu was crossing the river on a small boat. As he was setting out, he wasn't paying attention and the sword he had been carrying fell into the river. Because this man from the Kingdom of Chu had urgent business to take care of on the other side, he didn't jump into the water right away to find his sword. Instead, in order to remember where the sword had dropped, he carved a mark into the side of the boat. This is where the sword dropped into the water, he said to himself.　Then he crossed the river to take care of his affairs. On his way back, the man from the Kingdom of Chu looked for his sword in the water just under the mark on his boat. He looked here and there but he never found a thing.

Mencius' Mother Moves Three Times

In ancient China, there lived a great philosopher called Mencius. Mencius was Confucius' student. Mencius' mother was very careful about her child's education. She wanted her child to learn well while he was still small. Mencius' mother was also very concerned about their living environment because it could have such an enormous influence on a young child.

It is said that when Mencius was a boy, he was very good at copying other people's characteristics. As soon as he learned them, he knew them. One day Mencius' mother saw Mencius imitating the way relatives cried at a person's death. She thought that having a house in the vicinity of a grave was bad for her child. Everyday Mencius saw funerals and he learned all about the funeral proceedings. So his mother decided to move and leave the place where they had been living.

They moved to a new place. This time their house was near a vegetable market. Mencius' mother soon discovered that her son was learning how to do business and she decided that this place was no good either. Again they left where they were living to move to a new place.

This time they moved near a school. Mencius started imitating the way people studied. He started to study, to write, and he turned into a quiet person. This time Mencius' mother was content with the location. Mencius turned into a scholarly person and ended up being very famous.

附錄一　本書使用頻率最高的 500 個字

出現次數		和	160	都	103	東	66	己	51
的	990	以	158	麼	103	會	66	什	51
了	483	大	149	帝	95	自	65	每	51
他	402	生	143	要	94	開	64	做	51
是	380	們	140	常	94	好	63	著	51
人	364	說	140	方	93	見	61	你	50
有	347	裏	134	看	85	道	61	活	50
個	300	可	130	太	84	樣	61	最	50
就	284	家	130	皇	80	書	60	用	49
不	256	去	125	起	80	王	59	回	49
很	242	小	123	得	77	非	59	從	49
這	238	中	118	把	76	女	57	情	49
來	233	候	118	下	75	叫	56	發	49
上	206	地	116	打	74	老	56	經	49
在	203	多	116	能	73	出	55	孔	48
國	202	後	114	我	71	過	55	西	48
子	198	也	112	所	71	知	54	親	48
時	194	事	109	想	71	還	54	水	47
天	169	沒	107	那	68	年	53	字	47
到	160	爲	107	因	66	又	52	成	47

作	47	意	36	再	31	帶	24	教	20
法	47	邊	36	次	31	許	24	源	20
學	47	歡	36	思	31	當	24	管	20
孩	46	果	35	歷	31	希	23	寫	20
變	46	問	35	史	30	孟	23	仗	19
高	45	被	35	病	30	故	23	但	19
然	45	喜	35	第	30	望	23	郎	19
名	44	媽	35	結	30	猴	23	氣	19
吃	44	讀	35	辦	30	話	23	幾	19
她	44	古	34	找	29	路	23	歲	19
死	44	走	34	醫	29	遠	23	萬	19
別	44	界	34	呢	28	離	23	錢	19
些	44	記	34	千	27	化	22	白	18
面	44	傳	34	文	27	李	22	如	18
魚	44	心	33	兩	27	陀	22	放	18
聽	44	父	33	光	26	前	22	泥	18
住	43	母	33	而	26	華	22	船	18
世	42	明	33	位	26	頭	22	像	18
對	41	陽	33	種	26	友	21	操	18
兒	40	興	33	織	26	助	21	工	17
給	39	讓	33	牛	25	隻	21	夫	17
始	38	只	32	代	25	幫	21	正	17
花	38	長	32	外	25	先	20	仲	17
山	37	怎	32	黃	25	使	20	告	17
才	37	神	32	愚	25	朋	20	怕	17
曹	37	覺	32	已	24	河	20	服	17
現	37	公	31	哥	24	玩	20	武	17
弟	36	它	31	真	24	桃	20	直	17

飛	17	坐	15	美	13	磨	12	響	10
晚	17	身	15	座	13	總	12	土	9
造	17	倉	15	特	13	麗	12	今	9
堯	17	草	15	蛋	13	分	11	仙	9
朝	17	梨	15	答	13	少	11	平	9
訴	17	該	15	請	13	物	11	矛	9
農	17	慢	15	整	13	便	11	共	9
樹	17	頡	15	鮑	13	盾	11	同	9
點	17	本	14	題	13	條	11	后	9
藥	17	件	14	口	12	舜	11	安	9
蘇	17	其	14	月	12	漢	11	豆	9
久	16	拿	14	木	12	滿	11	刺	9
決	16	秦	14	北	12	影	11	往	9
叔	16	動	14	奴	12	融	11	治	9
定	16	郭	14	匈	12	火	10	紀	9
岳	16	媧	14	佛	12	丕	10	羿	9
易	16	畫	14	車	12	永	10	袋	9
卻	16	越	14	挖	12	完	10	喝	9
城	16	搬	14	重	12	更	10	植	9
姜	16	藏	14	哭	12	並	10	等	9
容	16	難	14	射	12	爸	10	嗎	9
狼	16	牙	13	海	12	近	10	擋	9
接	16	且	13	救	12	務	10	燈	9
章	16	民	13	間	12	殺	10	聲	9
跑	16	百	13	需	12	習	10	繩	9
應	16	快	13	熱	12	詩	10	手	8
力	15	珍	13	箭	12	盤	10	早	8
石	15	突	13	機	12	雖	10	受	8

相	8	倒	7	息	6	破	5	之	4
借	8	原	7	將	6	紋	5	布	4
婚	8	孫	7	笨	6	送	5	目	4
掉	8	針	7	鹿	6	追	5	各	4
理	8	釣	7	麻	6	馬	5	行	4
部	8	黑	7	備	6	累	5	吧	4
睡	8	搶	7	棒	6	處	5	忘	4
談	8	跟	7	飯	6	雪	5	里	4
關	8	龍	7	準	6	湖	5	姐	4
丈	7	聰	7	照	6	進	5	尙	4
反	7	繼	7	遇	6	雲	5	注	4
日	7	續	7	福	6	塗	5	油	4
比	7	轟	7	認	6	新	5	附	4
另	7	鐵	7	稻	6	楚	5	信	4
印	7	功	6	賣	6	溥	5	屋	4
向	7	田	6	燒	6	煩	5	急	4
吳	7	江	6	休	5	罪	5	洞	4
奇	7	羊	6	全	5	實	5	背	4
底	7	男	6	收	5	儀	5	剛	4
怪	7	育	6	衣	5	糊	5	留	4
社	7	兔	6	求	5	螢	5	站	4
度	7	幸	6	姓	5	錯	5		
流	7	南	6	或	5	牆	5		
禹	7	宮	6	表	5	蟲	5		
軍	7	差	6	亮	5	類	5		

附錄二　本書用詞整理

本書將前述500個常用字加以組合後，整理出下列約300個詞，希望能讓讀者在學習中文時，能有所幫助。

附录三 常用300个词

本书将500个常用字以组合後，整理出下列约300个词，按照拼音顺序排列，字後是页次。

20% Off
or More ?

BIGI 公司是一家從事中文學習教材的出版公司，我們將提供您一系列學習中文的的教材，在我們公司所出版的書中您將感受到高品質的中文圖書。

只要填好下列表格，我們公司將在每一本新書問世前，主動提供一個給您"嚐鮮"的機會，您可以用意想不到的折扣，買到新書！

機會不多，只有一萬個名額。

您也可以在 Internet 上按照我們的問題，直接填表寄回。
（http://www.bigiintl.com　E-mail: bigiintl@sprintmail.com　）

BIGI 讀者俱樂部申請表

Name	
Address	
Tel〔day〕	Tel〔night〕
Fax	
E-mail	
Please write down below if **you are a Chinese teacher?**	
School Name	
School Address	
School phone	